The Mathematics of
PERSONAL FINANCE & INVESTMENTS

Table of Contents

Introduction 4

Part I: Math Skills and Concepts

Pre-Skills Test..8
Adding and Subtracting Whole Numbers
   and Decimals..10
Multiplying and Dividing Whole Numbers
   and Decimals... 11
Fractions, Decimals, and Percents..............14
Problem Solving Strategy: Interpreting
   Data from Tables and Graphs 18
Mean, Median, and Mode 20
Basic Operations on a Calculator 22
Computing Mentally 24
Estimating Sums and Differences...............26
Estimating Products and Quotients 28
Problem Solving Strategy:
   Which Way to Compute?..........................30
Part I Review 32
Part I Test 34

Part II: Personal Finance

Pre-Skills Test...37
Sales Tax 40
Purchasing Power 43
Fixed and Variable Expenses 47
Budgeting Expenses 51
Problem Solving Application: Budgeting......55
The Cost of Raising a Family 59
Determining Net Worth.................................63
Decision Making: Developing a Budget.......67
Decision Making: Adjusting a Budget..........69
Money Tips 1 71
Calculator: Finding What Percent
   One Number Is of Another......................73
Part II Review 75
Part II Test 77

Contents
The Mathematics of Personal Finance and Investment, SV 9780547625683

Part III: Investments

Pre-Skills Test.................................79
U.S. Savings Bonds.............................81
Certificates of Deposit........................85
Corporate Stocks 89
Problem Solving Application:
    Trading Stocks.............................93
Corporate and Municipal Bonds 95
Mutual Funds...................................99
Retirement Plans 103
Problem Solving Strategy:
    Working Backward..........................109
Decision Making: Buying Stocks 113
Money Tips 2................................. 117
Estimation Skill: Overestimates
    and Underestimates of Products
    and Quotients 119
Problem Solving Strategy:
    Solving a Simpler Problem 121
Part III Review 125
Part III Test 127

Support Materials

Group Projects 130
Practice Forms 134
Charts..138
Glossary 145
Answer Key....................................151

Introduction

The **Consumer Math** series is designed to help consumers understand mathematics as it relates to their everyday lives. Activities in this series help students not only understand the underlying mathematical concepts and equations they encounter day to day, but also helps them to be more financially savvy.

Each workbook in the series is divided into three sections and begins with a basic review of math concepts before moving on to more specific topics. Each section includes the following: Pre-Skills Test, Problem Solving Strategies, a Review, and a Test.

In addition, each workbook includes the following support material: Group projects, Practice forms, Charts, a Glossary, and an Answer Key.

The Mathematics of Personal Finance and Investments

The Mathematics of Personal Finance and Investments covers math principles needed to plan a budget and build savings for retirement. Part I serves as a basic review of fundamental math concepts. Part II focuses on understanding how to plan for expenses and determine net worth. Part III concentrates on different types of investment tools used to build up savings for the future.

Part I: Math Skills and Concepts
- Whole Numbers
- Fractions, Decimals, & Percents
- Mean, Median, & Mode
- Basic Operations on a Calculator
- Computing Mentally
- Estimating

Part II: Personal Finance
- Sales Tax
- Purchasing Power
- Fixed and Variable Expenses
- Budgeting Expenses
- The Cost of Raising a Family
- Determining Net Worth
- Money Tips

Part III: Investments
- U.S. Savings Bonds
- Certificates of Deposit
- Corporate Stocks
- Corporate & Municipal Bonds
- Mutual Funds
- Pension Plans
- Money Tips

Comprehensive Lessons

A **Pre-Skills Test** preceding each section helps teachers evaluate students' abilities and determine learning needs before beginning the lessons.

A wide variety of relevant exercises and activities engage students and keep them interested. Examples are motivated through real-world applications. Exercises include individual skills practice, mixed practice, and application problems.

Extension features offer more challenging problems related to the lesson's theme. **Calculator** activities present problems in which using a calculator is advantageous over paper and pencil. Interesting, real-life problems in **Think About It** spur class participation and provide additional opportunities to assess students' understanding.

Focused review and assessment opportunities are also included for each section.

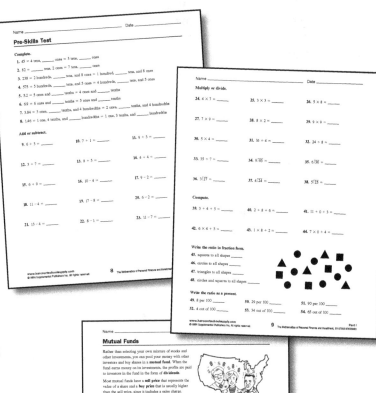

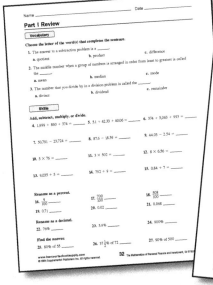

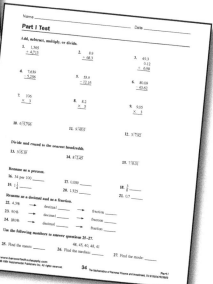

Extension Features

Money Tips examines the practical issues that affect buying decisions. Students look at factors that influence the cost of consumer goods as well as those that create consumer demand.

Mental Math helps students develop techniques to solve problems without using paper and pencil while reinforcing their confidence and estimation skills.

Estimation Skills extends students' understanding of estimation techniques and underscores their utility and practicality.

Calculator activities teach the keys and functions commonly available on calculators and emphasize the time-saving benefits.

A Strong Base in Problem Solving

Multiple **Problem Solving Applications** in each book relate math skills to people, careers, and the world around us. Applications throughout the series address consumer topics, such as renting apartments and finding miles per gallon, and careers, such as pharmacist and carpenter, which require the use of math skills.

Each **Problem Solving Strategy** presents a realistic problem, a strategy, and a step-by-step approach to solving the problem. Practice exercises reinforce the strategy. Strategies include Drawing a Diagram, Using Estimation, Using a Map, and Working Backward.

Decision Making features offer open-ended lessons that reinforce logical reasoning and move beyond computation to a consideration of factors involved in making sound decisions. Lessons in the *Consumer Math* series include Choosing Transportation, Developing a Budget, Buying Stocks, and Choosing the Correct Tax Form.

Support Materials

Group Projects

Practice Forms

Charts

Glossary

Answer Key

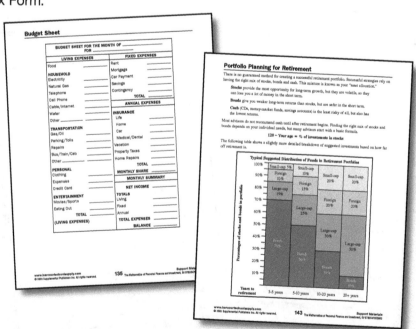

The Mathematics of Personal Finance and Investment, SV 9780547625683

Part I:
Math Skills and Concepts

Pre-Skills Test

Complete.

1. 45 = 4 tens, _____ ones = 3 tens, _____ ones

2. 82 = _____ tens, 2 ones = 7 tens, _____ ones

3. 238 = 2 hundreds, _____ tens, and 8 ones = 1 hundred, _____ tens, and 8 ones

4. 575 = 5 hundreds, _____ tens, and 5 ones = 4 hundreds, _____ tens, and 5 ones

5. 5.2 = 5 ones and _____ tenths = 4 ones and _____ tenths

6. 6.9 = 6 ones and _____ tenths = 5 ones and _____ tenths

7. 3.84 = 3 ones, _____ tenths, and 4 hundredths = 2 ones, _____ tenths, and 4 hundredths

8. 1.46 = 1 one, 4 tenths, and _____ hundredths = 1 one, 3 tenths, and _____ hundredths

Add or subtract.

9. $6 + 3 =$ _____

10. $7 + 1 =$ _____

11. $9 + 3 =$ _____

12. $3 + 7 =$ _____

13. $8 + 5 =$ _____

14. $4 + 4 =$ _____

15. $6 + 9 =$ _____

16. $10 - 4 =$ _____

17. $9 - 2 =$ _____

18. $11 - 4 =$ _____

19. $17 - 8 =$ _____

20. $6 - 2 =$ _____

21. $13 - 4 =$ _____

22. $8 - 1 =$ _____

23. $11 - 7 =$ _____

Name _____ Date _____

Multiply or divide.

24. $4 \times 7 =$ _____

25. $3 \times 3 =$ _____

26. $5 \times 8 =$ _____

27. $7 \times 9 =$ _____

28. $8 \times 2 =$ _____

29. $9 \times 9 =$ _____

30. $5 \times 4 =$ _____

31. $16 \div 4 =$ _____

32. $24 \div 8 =$ _____

33. $35 \div 7 =$ _____

34. $9\overline{)63} =$ _____

35. $6\overline{)36} =$ _____

36. $3\overline{)27} =$ _____

37. $4\overline{)24} =$ _____

38. $5\overline{)25} =$ _____

Compute.

39. $3 + 4 + 5 =$ _____

40. $2 + 8 + 6 =$ _____

41. $11 + 0 + 3 =$ _____

42. $6 \times 4 + 3 =$ _____

43. $1 \times 8 + 2 =$ _____

44. $7 \times 0 + 4 =$ _____

Write the ratio in fraction form.

45. squares to all shapes _____

46. circles to all shapes _____

47. triangles to all shapes _____

48. circles and squares to all shapes _____

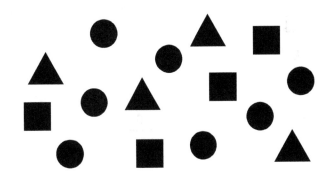

Write the ratio as a percent.

49. 8 per 100 _____

50. 29 per 100 _____

51. 90 per 100 _____

52. 4 out of 100 _____

53. 34 out of 100 _____

54. 65 out of 100 _____

The Mathematics of Personal Finance and Investment, SV 9780547625683

Name _____ Date _____

Adding and Subtracting Whole Numbers and Decimals

Addition and subtraction are related operations.

> Addend + Addend = Sum   Sum − Addend = Addend (= Difference)

Skill 1   Adding or subtracting whole numbers

(1a) Add 4,068 + 5,794

Step 1	**Step 2**	**Step 3**	**Step 4**
Add ones. Regroup.	Add tens. Regroup.	Add hundreds.	Add thousands.
$\begin{array}{r} \overset{1}{} \\ 4,068 \\ +\,5,794 \\ \hline 2 \end{array}$	$\begin{array}{r} \overset{1\ 1}{} \\ 4,068 \\ +\,5,794 \\ \hline 62 \end{array}$	$\begin{array}{r} \overset{1\ 1}{} \\ 4,068 \\ +\,5,794 \\ \hline 862 \end{array}$	$\begin{array}{r} \overset{1\ 1}{} \\ 4,068 \\ +\,5,794 \\ \hline 9,862 \end{array}$

(1b) Subtract 8,674 − 6,319

Step 1	**Step 2**	**Step 3**	**Step 4**
Regroup tens. Subtract ones.	Subtract tens.	Subtract hundreds.	Subtract thousands.
$\begin{array}{r} \overset{6\ 14}{8,67\!\!\!/4} \\ -\,6,319 \\ \hline 5 \end{array}$	$\begin{array}{r} \overset{6\ 14}{8,67\!\!\!/4} \\ -\,6,319 \\ \hline 55 \end{array}$	$\begin{array}{r} \overset{6\ 14}{8,67\!\!\!/4} \\ -\,6,319 \\ \hline 355 \end{array}$	$\begin{array}{r} \overset{6\ 14}{8,67\!\!\!/4} \\ -\,6,319 \\ \hline 2,355 \end{array}$

Skill 2   Respect the position of the decimal point when adding or subtracting.

Subtract: 9.2 − 0.7

Step 1	**Step 2**	**Step 3**	**Step 4**
Line up the decimal points.	Write the decimal point for the difference.	Regroup ones. Subtract tenths.	Subtract ones.
$\begin{array}{r} 9.2 \\ -\,0.7 \\ \hline \end{array}$	$\begin{array}{r} 9.2 \\ -\,0.7 \\ \hline . \end{array}$	$\begin{array}{r} \overset{8\ 12}{9\!\!\!/.2} \\ -\,0.7 \\ \hline .5 \end{array}$	$\begin{array}{r} \overset{8\ 12}{9\!\!\!/.2} \\ -\,0.7 \\ \hline 8.5 \end{array}$

> **TIP** When lining up decimals, add zero as a placeholder, if necessary.
>
> Add 5.16 + 8.7 + 4.02
>
> $\begin{array}{r} 5.16 \\ 8.70 \\ +\,4.02 \\ \hline 17.88 \end{array}$

Multiplying and Dividing Whole Numbers and Decimals

Factor $\times$ Factor = Product   Dividend $\div$ Divisor = Quotient and (R) Remainder

$$\begin{array}{r} \text{Factor} \\ \times \quad \text{Factor} \\ \hline \text{Product} \end{array}$$

$$\text{Divisor} \overline{)\text{Dividend}}^{\text{Quotient (R) Remainder}}$$

Skill 1   **Multiplying whole numbers**

Step 1

Multiply ones. Regroup.

$$\begin{array}{r} \overset{6}{4}07 \\ \times \quad 9 \\ \hline 3 \end{array}$$

Step 2

Multiply tens. Than add 6 tens.
THINK: 0 tens + 6 tens = 6 tens

$$\begin{array}{r} 4\overset{6}{0}7 \\ \times \quad 9 \\ \hline 63 \end{array}$$

Step 3

Multiply hundreds.

$$\begin{array}{r} 4\overset{6}{0}7 \\ \times \quad 9 \\ \hline 3,663 \end{array}$$

Skill 2   **Multiplying whole numbers and decimals**

Step 1

Multiply as you would whole numbers.

$$\begin{array}{r} 1.73 \\ \times \quad 8 \\ \hline 1384 \end{array}$$

Step 2

Count the number of decimal places in the factors.
There are that many decimal places in the product.

$$\begin{array}{r} 1.73 \\ \times \quad 8 \\ \hline 13.84 \end{array}$$
2 decimal places
0 decimal places
2 decimal places

Skill 3   **Dividing decimals by whole numbers**

Step 1 Place the decimal point in the quotient directly above the decimal point in the dividend.

Step 2 Divide as you would whole numbers. Write additional zeros in the dividend as needed.

$$\begin{array}{r} 0.485 \\ 7\overline{)3,400} \\ \underline{28}\!\downarrow \\ 60 \\ \underline{56}\!\downarrow \\ 40 \\ \underline{35} \\ 5 \end{array}$$

> **TIP** **Rounding the quotient:** Remember: $\approx$ means approximately equal to.
>
> **Rounding to the hundredths** $0.485 \approx 0.49$
> **Rounding to the tenths** $0.485 \approx 0.5$

11

Practice

Add, subtract, multiply, or divide.

1. $\begin{array}{r} 5.8 \\ + 52.96 \\ \hline \end{array}$

2. $\begin{array}{r} 135 \\ 644 \\ + 12 \\ \hline \end{array}$

3. $\begin{array}{r} 46.5 \\ 47.08 \\ + 0.4 \\ \hline \end{array}$

4. $\begin{array}{r} 8{,}004 \\ - 6{,}452 \\ \hline \end{array}$

5. $\begin{array}{r} 92.8 \\ - 67.51 \\ \hline \end{array}$

6. $\begin{array}{r} 78.54 \\ - 65.6 \\ \hline \end{array}$

7. $\begin{array}{r} 902 \\ \times \ \ 8 \\ \hline \end{array}$

8. $\begin{array}{r} 6.5 \\ \times \ 6 \\ \hline \end{array}$

9. $\begin{array}{r} 4.04 \\ \times \ \ 7 \\ \hline \end{array}$

10. $5\overline{)60}$

11. $4\overline{)0.8}$

12. $8\overline{)3.76}$

13. $7{,}125 + 7{,}908 = $ _____

14. $5{,}086 + 13 + 496 = $ _____

15. $2.9 + 47.08 + 40 = $ _____

16. $753 - 258 = $ _____

17. $81.65 - 52.87 = $ _____

18. $90.01 - 22.32 = $ _____

19. $6 \times 554 = $ _____

20. $5 \times 0.98 = $ _____

21. $7 \times 0.02 = $ _____

22. $56 \div 6 = $ _____

23. $9{,}320 \div 2 = $ _____

24. $45.71 \div 7 = $ _____

Divide and round to the nearest tenth.

25. $2.25 \div 7 = $ _____

26. $8.71 \div 5 = $ _____

Divide and round to the nearest hundredth.

27. $5.82 \div 9 = $ _____

28. $9.13 \div 4 = $ _____

Solve.

29. It is 1,835 miles from Seattle, Washington, to Kansas City, Missouri, and 1,238 miles from Kansas City to Orlando, Florida. How many miles is it total from Seattle to Kansas City and then on to Orlando? _____

30. Gilbert spent $51.69 at the hardware store and $49.02 at the garden center. How much did he spend all together? _____

31. It is 1,238 miles from New York City to Omaha, Nebraska. You have already traveled 925 miles. How many more miles do you need to travel? _____

32. You need to buy some paintbrushes. The total cost of the paintbrushes is $12.09. You have $9.21. How much more money do you need? _____

33. It is 638 miles from Boston to Philadelphia and back again. You made this trip 6 times. How many miles did you travel in all? _____

34. Your class is selling school mugs for $13.25 each. The class sold 7 mugs during the first hour of the sale. How much money was collected during that hour? _____

35. A 28-oz box of cereal costs $3.36. How much is the cost per ounce? _____

36. It is about 2,198 miles from Las Vegas, Nevada, to Charlotte, North Carolina. You made the trip in 7 days, traveling the same distance each day. How many miles did you travel each day? _____

Fractions, Decimals, and Percents

Skill 1   Renaming decimals as percents

Rename 0.9 as a percent.

| **Step 1** | Multiply by 100 by moving the decimal point 2 places to the right. Write additional zeros if necessary. | 0.90 ⟶ 90.0 |
| **Step 2** | Write the percent sign. | 90% |

Other examples

0.89 ⟶ 0.89 ⟶ 89%   0.034 ⟶ 0.034 ⟶ 3.4%   8.4 ⟶ 8.40 ⟶ 840%

Skill 2   Renaming fractions as percents

Rename $\frac{1}{5}$ as a percent.

| **Step 1** | Write the fraction as a decimal. Divide the numerator by the denominator. Write additional zeros if necessary. | $\frac{1}{5}$ ⟶ $5\overline{)1.0}^{\,0.2}$ |
| **Step 2** | Write the decimal as a percent. | 0.20 ⟶ 20% |

Skill 3   Renaming percents as decimals

Rename 3% as a decimal.

| **Step 1** | Divide by 100 by moving the decimal point 2 places to the left. Write additional zeros if necessary. | 3% ⟶ 0.03% |
| **Step 2** | Remove the percent sign. | 0.03 |

Other examples

43% ⟶ 0.4 3% ⟶ 0.43   5.7% ⟶ 0.0 5.7% ⟶ 0.057   287% ⟶ 2.8 7% ⟶ 2.87

Skill 4   **Renaming percents as fractions**

Rename 80% as a fraction.

| **Step 1** | Write the percent as a fraction with a denominator of 100. | $80\% = \dfrac{80}{100}$ |

| **Step 2** | Write the fraction in lowest terms. | $\dfrac{80}{100} = \dfrac{80 \div 20}{100 \div 20} = \dfrac{4}{5}$ |

Other examples

$75\% = \dfrac{75}{100} = \dfrac{75 \div 25}{100 \div 25} = \dfrac{3}{4}$
$\qquad$
$150\% = \dfrac{150}{100} = \dfrac{150 \div 50}{100 \div 50} = \dfrac{3}{2} = 1\dfrac{1}{2}$

Skill 5   **Expressing percents as decimals**

Any percent can be expressed as a decimal.

Find 40% of 19.

| **Step 1** | Write the problem as a number sentence. | 40% of 19 is _____ $\longrightarrow$ 40% $\times$ 19 = _____ |

| **Step 2** | Rename the percent as a decimal. **THINK:** $40\% = 0.40 = 0.4$ | $0.4 \times 19 =$ _____ |

| **Step 3** | Solve. | $0.4 \times 19 = 7.6$ |

Skill 6   **Expressing percents as fractions**

Sometimes it is easier to express a percent as a fraction.

Find 75% of 16.

| **Step 1** | Write the problem as a number sentence. | 75% of 16 is _____ $\longrightarrow$ 75% $\times$ 16 = _____ |

| **Step 2** | Rename the percent as a fraction. **THINK:** $75\% = \dfrac{3}{4}$ | $\dfrac{3}{4} \times 16 =$ _____ |

| **Step 3** | Solve. **THINK:** $\dfrac{1}{4} \times 16 \longrightarrow 16 \div 4 = 4$ $\dfrac{3}{4} \times 16 \longrightarrow 3 \times 4 = 12$ $\dfrac{3}{4} \times 16 = 12$ So 75% of 16 is 12. | |

Practice

Rename as a percent.

1. $\frac{56}{100}$ = _____

2. $\frac{4}{100}$ = _____

3. $\frac{119}{100}$ = _____

4. 0.96 = _____

5. 0.081 = _____

6. 2 = _____

Rename as a decimal and as a percent.

7. $\frac{1}{8}$ = _____ = _____

8. $\frac{3}{4}$ = _____ = _____

9. $\frac{4}{5}$ = _____ = _____

10. $5\frac{3}{10}$ = _____ = _____

11. $6\frac{1}{2}$ = _____ = _____

12. $2\frac{5}{8}$ = _____ = _____

Rename as a decimal.

13. 57% = _____

14. 41% = _____

15. 5% = _____

16. 9.1% = _____

17. 0.08% = _____

18. 161% = _____

Rename as a fraction. Write fractions in lowest terms.

19. 10% = _____

20. 80% = _____

21. 55% = _____

22. 140% = _____

23. 113% = _____

24. 308% = _____

Find the answer. Decide whether to express the percent as a decimal or as a fraction.

25. 40% of 70 = _____

26. 75% of 36 = _____

27. 50% of 80 = _____

28. 70% of 45 = _____

29. 25% of 88 = _____

30. $66\frac{2}{3}\%$ of 63 = _____

31. $37\frac{1}{2}\%$ of 80 = _____

32. 80% of 36 = _____

33. $83\frac{1}{3}\%$ of 72 = _____

34. $12\frac{1}{2}\%$ of 96 = _____

35. 5% of 28 = _____

36. $33\frac{1}{3}\%$ of 42 = _____

Solve.

37. The trip between two cities is exactly 120 miles. You have gone 70% of this distance. How far have you gone? _____

38. David received a grade of 95% on his science test. There were 60 multiple-choice questions on the test. How many questions did David get correct? _____

39. It takes Edward 60 minutes to mow the lawn. It takes Rebecca 75% of Edward's time. How long does it take Rebecca? _____

40. A bicycle originally cost $318. It is now being sold for 65% of its original price. How much does the bicycle cost now? _____

41. A mobile phone originally cost $490. It is now being sold at 20% off. How much has been deducted from the original cost of the mobile phone? _____

42. In an election poll, 45% of the 120 people interviewed said that they voted for Mike Langham for mayor. The rest said that they voted for Ashley Mancia.

a. How many people said they voted for Mike Langham? _____

b. How many people said they voted for Ashley Mancia? _____

Problem Solving Strategy: Interpreting Data from Tables and Graphs

Situation:

The sales staff at Donney Motors keeps records of their car and truck sales. Contests are sometimes held to encourage special efforts to sell various cars and trucks. How can these records be used to identify a salesperson's performance?

Strategy:

You can use information in a **table** or a **bar graph** to solve a problem.

Applying the Strategy:

A. The salesperson who sold the greatest number of trucks in October won a flat-screen TV. Who was it?

THINK: Look at the column labeled "Number of Trucks Sold."

October Sales	
Salesperson	**Number of Trucks Sold**
Ruth	22
Art	15
John	9
Eric	12
Mindy	4

Step 1 Which number is the greatest?
(22)

Step 2 Which name is on the same line as 22?
(Ruth)

Ruth sold the greatest number of trucks in October and won the TV.

B. Eric sold the greatest number of cars and trucks last year and won a free trip. How many cars and trucks did he sell?

THINK: Look at the bar above Eric's name.

Step 1 Between which 2 numbers does the bar lie?
(250 and 300)

Step 2 Is the bar nearer to 250 or 300?
(It is halfway between 250 and 300.)

Step 3 What number is halfway between 250 and 300?
(250 + 300 = 550)
(550 ÷ 2 = 275)

Eric sold 275 cars and trucks last year.

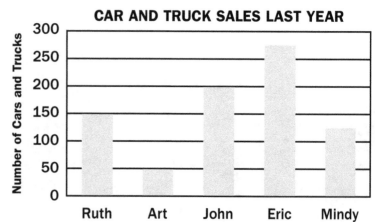

CAR AND TRUCK SALES LAST YEAR

Name _____ Date _____

Practice

Use the table of December sales for problems 1–2.

1. How many cars did Ginger sell? _____

2. How many more cars did Art sell than Eric?

_____

December Sales	
Salesperson	**Number of Cars Sold**
Ruth	10
Art	25
John	35
Ginger	25
Eric	20
Mindy	20

The sales staff posted a bar graph to show the numbers of cars and trucks Donney Motors leased last year. Use the bar graph to answer problems 3–4.

3. How many hatchbacks were leased? _____

4. How many more SUVs were leased than 2-door sedans?

_____

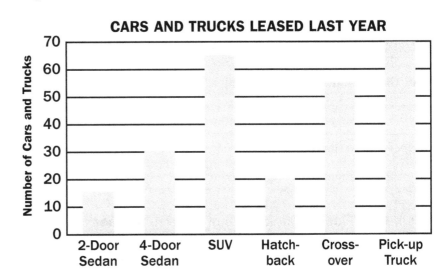

5. Use the information in the "December Sales" table at the top of the page to construct a bar graph. Use this vertical scale: 0, 5, 10, 15, 20, 25, 30, 35.

_____

Mean, Median, and Mode

> **Mean (average)**—The sum of a group of numbers divided by the number of addends.
> **Median**—The middle number when a group of numbers is arranged in order from least to greatest.
> **Mode**—The number that occurs most frequently in a group of numbers.

Skill 1 Finding the mean

Find the mean of these basketball players' scores: 48, 36, 51, 72, 58.

| Step 1 | Add the scores. | $48 + 36 + 51 + 72 + 58 = 265$ |
| Step 2 | Divide by the number of scores. | $265 \div 5 = 53$ |

The mean, or average, of these scores is 53.

Skill 2 Finding the median of an odd number of scores

Find the median of these bowling scores: 126, 108, 145, 108, 117.

| Step 1 | Arrange the scores in order. | 108   108   117   126   145 |
| Step 2 | Find the middle score. | 117 |

The median of these scores is 117.

Skill 3 Finding the median of an even number of scores

Find the median of these bowling scores: 139, 106, 145, 113, 128, 109.

Step 1	Arrange the scores in order.	106 109 113 128 139 145
Step 2	Find the middle score. (**THINK:** There is no *one* middle number.)	113 128
Step 3	Find the mean of the two middle scores.	$113 + 128 = 241 \div 2 = 120.5$

The median of these scores is 120.5.

Skill 4 Finding the mode

Find the mode of these race times: 9.3, 9.6, 9.2, 10.2, 9.6, 10.1, 9.5.

Find the time that occurs most often.   9.6 occurs twice

The mode of these scores is 9.6.

Name _____ Date _____

Practice

Find the mean.

1. 19, 20, 27 _____

2. 7.5, 1.9, 5.9 _____

3. 435, 880, 526, 747 _____

4. 28, 96, 43, 105 _____

5. 50, 41, 41, 40, 48 _____

6. 0.41, 0.78, 0.67, 0.84, 0.55 _____

Find the median.

7. 10, 46, 58, 79, 31 _____

8. 12, 45, 30, 57, 41 _____

9. 4.6, 9.5, 1.2, 5.7, 8.9 _____

10. 8.3, 8.5, 7.3, 4.9, 7.5, 10.6 _____

Find the mode.

11. 4, 6, 8, 2, 5, 9, 2, 1 _____

12. 2.9, 7.8, 4.1, 7.3, 9.3, 4.1, 6.5 _____

Find the mean, the median, and the mode. Round the mean and median to the nearest tenth.

13. 89, 31, 25   mean _____   median _____   mode _____

14. 9.6, 5.8, 10.4   mean _____   median _____   mode _____

15. 605, 550, 550, 501   mean _____   median _____   mode _____

16. 38, 26, 12, 38, 17   mean _____   median _____   mode _____

17. 9.4, 8.2, 7.5, 8.2, 10.3   mean _____   median _____   mode _____

Solve.

18. The high temperatures last week were 89°F, 92°F, 90°F, 89°F, 85°F, 87°F, and 84°F. What are the mean, median, and mode of these temperatures?

mean _____   median _____   mode _____

Extension   **Using a Tally**

Each time Ed played miniature golf, he made a tally mark next to his score.

1. How many games did Ed play? _____

2. What are his two mode scores? _____

3. What is his median score? _____

4. What is the total of the scores of:
   (a) 69? _____; (b) 68? _____; (c) 67? _____

5. What is his mean score? _____

Score	Total	Score	Total
72 - I	72	69 - ℍ IIII	
71 - III	213	68 - IIII	
70 - ℍ IIII	630	67 - II	

Basic Operations on a Calculator

When you want to compute quickly and accurately with greater numbers, you can use a calculator.

The four basic operations (addition, subtraction, multiplication, and division) can be performed easily.

Operation	Calculator Entry	Calculator Display
Add: 49,567 + 78,078	[4] [9] [5] [6] [7] [+] [7] [8] [0] [7] [8] [=]	127,645
Subtract: 34.014 − 5.708	[3] [4] [.] [0] [1] [4] [−] [5] [.] [7] [0] [8] [=]	28.306
Multiply: 908 × 0.045	[9] [0] [8] [×] [0] [.] [0] [4] [5] [=]	40.86
Divide: 4.9452 ÷ 0.078	[4] [.] [9] [4] [5] [2] [÷] [0] [.] [0] [7] [8] [=]	63.4

You can use a calculator to do a series of operations without using the [=] **key (is equal to)** after each operation.

Operation	Calculator Entry	Calculator Display
1. Subtract.	[4] [5] [.] [0] [9] [−] [6] [+] ↑ Get ready to subtract.	39.09
2. Add.	[4] [.] [7] [−] ↑ Get ready to subtract.	43.79
3. Subtract.	[1] [8] [=]	25.79

So, 45.09 − 6 + 4.7 − 18 = 25.79.

> **TIP** The [CE] key (**Clear Entry**) can help you when you have entered a wrong number into the calculator.

Name _____ Date _____

1. For which operations will the order in which you enter two numbers not affect the answer? Why?

_____

_____

2. The entry below was made on two different calculators. One calculator displayed the answer 6.15. The other calculator displayed the answer 16.4. Explain the different answers.

[4] [.] [5] [×] [3] [+] [7] [−] [8] [.] [2] [÷] [2] [=]

_____

_____

Practice

Use a calculator to compute.

1. $4,527,811 - 679,416 =$ _____

2. $8,729 + 5,982 =$ _____

3. $50,832 \div 72 =$ _____

4. $368.1 - 68.968 =$ _____

5. $758.69 \times 41.6 =$ _____

6. $79.15 \times 10.06 \div 5 =$ _____

7. 69.5 divided into 98,273 = _____

8. 0.7 divided into 0.049 = _____

Divide and round to the nearest tenth.

9. $41.5\overline{)608}$

10. $6.02\overline{)796}$

Divide and round to the nearest hundredth.

11. $0.63 \div 5.2 =$ _____

12. $86.1\overline{)5.173}$

Compute from left to right.

13. $266.9 - 6.721 + 697.2 - 716.01 =$ _____

14. $63 \div 0.5 \times 0.64 \div 48 =$ _____

Solve.

15. A stadium has 50,086 seats. At the last game, 46,239 seats were filled. How many seats were empty?

_____

16. Cheryl saved the same amount each month for 24 months. At the end of the 24 months, she had saved a total of $5,148. How much did Cheryl save each month? _____

Name _____   Date _____

Computing Mentally

You may often find it easier to compute mentally than to use a pencil and paper or even a calculator. You can add mentally by using numbers that are **multiples of 10** and then adjusting.

Example 1: You are buying a shirt for $19 and a jacket for $44. Mentally compute the cost of the shirt and the jacket.

Add: $19 + $44
THINK: $19 is $1 less than $20. $20 + $44 = $64

So $19 + $44 is $1 less than $64, or $63.

The shirt and the jacket will cost $63.

You can subtract mentally in the same way.

Example 2: Subtract:
  a. 94 − 18
     THINK: 18 is 2 less than 20.

     94 − 20 = 74
     So 94 − 18 is 2 more than 74, or 76.

  b. 465 − 190
     THINK: 190 is 10 less than 200.

     465 − 200 = 265
     So 465 − 190 is 10 more than 265, or 275.

Mental computation is also commonly used when you multiply or divide by **powers of 10**, such as 10, 100, or 1,000.

Example 3: Multiply: 100×87.30
THINK: The product must be greater than 87.3, so move the decimal point to the right.

$100 \times 87.30 = 8,730$

2 zeros
   2 places right

Example 4: Divide: $38,430 \div 1,000$
THINK: The quotient must be less than 38,430, so move the decimal point to the left.

$38,430 \div 1,000 = 38.43$

3 places left
   3 zeros

The Mathematics of Personal Finance and Investment, SV 9780547625683

Name _____ Date _____

1. Ricky argues that mental computation is a waste of time, since he has a calculator. How would you convince Ricky that he is wrong?

_____

_____

Practice

Use mental computation to add or subtract.

1. $79 + 42 =$ _____

2. $58 + 15 =$ _____

3. $383 + 210 =$ _____

4. $59¢ + 32¢ =$ _____

5. $\$2.77 + \$5.90 =$ _____

6. $9.83 + 5.99 =$ _____

7. $73 - 49 =$ _____

8. $639 - 402 =$ _____

9. $80¢ - 41¢ =$ _____

10. $\$548 - \$180 =$ _____

11. $\$4.90 - \$0.31 =$ _____

12. $8.60 - 2.48 =$ _____

Use mental computation to multiply or divide.

13. $100 \times 9.1 =$ _____

14. $10 \times 63.57 =$ _____

15. $1,000 \times 0.76 =$ _____

16. $42.7 \div 10 =$ _____

17. $51.8 \div 100 =$ _____

18. $782 \div 1,000 =$ _____

Solve using mental computation.

19. A \$780 plane ticket is marked down by \$49. How much does the plane ticket now sell for?

_____

20. A stack of 100 CDs without cases has a mass of 1.5 kilograms. What is the mass in kilograms of each CD in the stack? _____

Multiplying mentally by 50 and by 25.

Multiply: 50×2.8
THINK: $100 \times 2.8 = 280$
Since $50 = 100 \div 2$, then $50 \times 2.8 = 280 \div 2 = 140$.

Multiply: 25×16.4
THINK: $100 \times 16.4 = 1,640$
Since $25 = 100 \div 4$, then $25 \times 16.4 = 1,640 \div 4 = 410$.

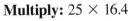

Use mental computation to multiply.

1. $50 \times 18 =$ _____

2. $25 \times 480 =$ _____

3. $50 \times 640 =$ _____

Estimating Sums and Differences

A common way to **estimate** sums is to round each number to the same **place value** and then add mentally.

Example 1: About how much is the total population of Fairview County?

Town	Greenfield	Salem	Goshen	Wells
Population	21,284	3,487	38,372	10,480

| **Step 1** | Round each number to the thousands place.

$$
\begin{array}{rcr}
21,284 & \longrightarrow & 21,000 \\
3,487 & \longrightarrow & 3,000 \\
38,372 & \longrightarrow & 38,000 \\
+\ 10,480 & \longrightarrow & +\ 10,000 \\
\hline
 & & 72,000
\end{array}
$$

| **Step 2** | Add.

72,000 is a good estimate for the total population.

Example 2:

a. Estimate: $31.07 + 0.6 + 3.87$

| **Step 1** | Round each number to the tenths place.

$$
\begin{array}{rcr}
31.07 & \longrightarrow & 31.1 \\
0.6 & \longrightarrow & 0.6 \\
+\ 3.87 & \longrightarrow & +\ 3.9 \\
\hline
 & & 35.6
\end{array}
$$

| **Step 2** | Add.

b. Estimate: $95¢ + \$2.09 + \$5.75$

| **Step 1** | Round each number to the ones place.

$$
\begin{array}{rcr}
\$0.95 & \longrightarrow & \$1 \\
\$2.09 & \longrightarrow & \$2 \\
+\ \$5.75 & \longrightarrow & +\ \$6 \\
\hline
 & & \$9
\end{array}
$$

| **Step 2** | Add.

The same estimating rules are used for subtraction.

Example 3:

a. Estimate: $27,387 - 2,163$

| **Step 1** | Round each number to the thousands place.

$$
\begin{array}{rcr}
27,387 & \longrightarrow & 27,000 \\
-\ 2,163 & \longrightarrow & -\ 2,000 \\
\hline
 & \longrightarrow & 25,000
\end{array}
$$

| **Step 2** | Subtract.

b. Estimate: $0.37 - 0.097$

| **Step 1** | Round each number to the tenths place.

$$
\begin{array}{rcr}
0.37 & \longrightarrow & 0.4 \\
-\ 0.097 & \longrightarrow & -\ 0.1 \\
\hline
 & \longrightarrow & 0.3
\end{array}
$$

| **Step 2** | Subtract.

Name _____ Date _____

Think About It

1. How is mental computation different from estimation?

_____

_____

2. To estimate $4.80 + $2.25 + $3.40, Gail used $5 + $2 + $3 = $10. Gail's mother rounded up and used $5 + $3 + 4 = $12. What are some advantages of doing estimation the second way?

_____

_____

Practice

Estimate the sum or difference.

1.   731 (hundreds)
     + 451

2.   835 (tens)
       951
     + 17

3. $9.17 (ones)
     + $6.47

4. $5.42 (ones)
       $0.28
     + $4.65

5.   126.8   (tens)
     + 63.38

6.   0.022 (hundredths)
     + 0.76

7.   73,897 (thousands)
     + 9,124

8.   0.051   (thousandths)
     + 0.0028

9.   765 (tens)
     − 42

10.   51,504 (ten thousands)
      − 13,880

11. $0.45 (tenths)
      − $0.16

12. $17.35 (ones)
      − $0.97

13.   571.5 (tens)
      − 57.2

14.   7.12 (tenths)
      − 0.38

15. $388.30 (tens)
      − $97.89

Solve.

16. Robert bought a T-shirt for $8.78. About how much change should he get from $20.00?

_____

17. A laptop is advertised at Westland Electronics for $732. The same laptop is on sale at KW Computing for $588. About how much can be saved by buying the laptop at KW Computing? _____

Estimating Products and Quotients

A common way to estimate products and quotients is to round each number to its **greatest place** and then compute mentally.

Example 1: There were 285 wildlife pamphlets left to be distributed. Six friends shared the task. About how many pamphlets must each person hand out if they share the job?

| **Step 1** | Round. | 285 rounds to 300. Since 6 is a 1-digit number, it does not need to be rounded. |

| **Step 2** | Divide. | 300 ÷ 6 = 50. |

So each person will hand out about 50 pamphlets.

Example 2:
a. Estimate: 2,789 × 48

| **Step 1** | Round. | 3,000 × 50 |
| **Step 2** | Multiply. | 150,000 |

b. Estimate: 22,270 ÷ 39

| **Step 1** | Round. | 20,000 ÷ 40 |
| **Step 2** | Divide. | 500 |

When multiplying or dividing decimals or money amounts, estimate by rounding each number to its **greatest nonzero place**.

Example 3:
a. Estimate: 78 × $0.29

| **Step 1** | Round. | 80 × $0.30 |
| **Step 2** | Multiply. | $24 |

b. Estimate: 324.8 ÷ 4.87

| **Step 1** | Round. | 300 ÷ 5 |
| **Step 2** | Divide. | 60 |

28
The Mathematics of Personal Finance and Investment, SV 9780547625683

Name _____ Date _____

Think About It

1. Laura calculated that 3.2 × 16.8 is 5.376. Estimate and explain why Laura's answer cannot be correct.

_____

_____

_____

Practice

Estimate the product and quotient.

1. 7,245 × 77 ≈ _____

2. 85 × $45.08 ≈ _____

3. 690 × $32.28 ≈ _____

4. 15 × 8.1 ≈ _____

5. 7.2 × 5.46 ≈ _____

6. 52.42 × 4.73 ≈ _____

7. 618 × $0.15 ≈ _____

8. 428 × 0.52 ≈ _____

9. 0.98 × 0.67 ≈ _____

10. 589 ÷ 62 ≈ _____

11. 838 ÷ 415 ≈ _____

12. $44.10 ÷ 8 ≈ _____

13. $76.90 ÷ 18 ≈ _____

14. $526 ÷ 46 ≈ _____

15. 13 ÷ 5.23 ≈ _____

16. 280.8 ÷ 59 ≈ _____

17. 68.3 ÷ 7.2 ≈ _____

18. 825.6 ÷ 42.5 ≈ _____

Use the menu for problems 19–20.

19. About how much will 8 hamburgers cost?

_____

20. About how many salads can be bought for $12.0? _____

MENU	
Hamburgers	$2.89
Hot Dogs	$2.15
Chicken Sandwich	$3.49
Salad	$2.50
Juice	$1.19
Apple Slices	$0.79
Popcorn	$0.75

Solve.

21. A hotel needs to buy 42 mattresses. The mattresses cost $329.50 each. About how much will the 42 mattresses cost? _____

22. Cell phone games cost $3.15 each. About how many cell phone games can be bought for $28.00?

_____

Name _____   Date _____

Problem Solving Strategy: Which Way to Compute?

Situation:

Suppose you are asked to find the cost of 5 pairs of socks at $1.95 a pair plus a sales tax of $0.40. Which way would you use to compute the answer?

Strategy:

Use paper and pencil skills, a calculator, or mental computation skills depending on the situation, the numbers involved, or your own personal preference.

Applying the Strategy:

Joan took out a pencil and computed:

Jill took out a calculator and computed:

$$
\begin{array}{r}
\$1.95 \\
\times \quad 5 \\
\hline
\$9.75 \\
+ \ 0.40 \\
\hline
\$10.15
\end{array}
$$

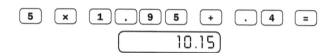

Jackie thought:

      $1.95 is 5¢ less than $2. So 5 pairs are 25¢ less than $10, or $9.75, plus 40¢.

      40¢ is 25¢ plus 15¢. So $9.75 plus 25¢ is $10, plus 15¢ is $10.15.

Notice that Joan, Jill, and Jackie all got the same answer.

Other Situations:

A. What is the best way to compute the amount of change that Ray received if he paid $5.00 for a $2.97 meal?

Ray can easily compute this mentally.
He thinks: $2.97 is 3¢ less than $3.00.
$5.00 − $3.00 is $2.00.

So $5.00 − $2.97 is $2.00 plus 3¢, or $2.03.

B. What is the best way for Alvin to compute the new balance in the class treasury? The balance was $357.82. He made a deposit of $182.14 and then made a withdrawal of $78.50.

Alvin needs an exact answer, and the numbers are too great to use mental computation. So he uses his calculator or paper and pencil to get $461.46.

C. What is the best way for Mr. Lee to compute the total length of pipe? One piece is $4\frac{3}{4}$ feet long, and the other is $2\frac{7}{8}$ feet long.

If Mr. Lee wants an exact answer, it is unlikely that he will use mental computation or convert to decimals and use a calculator. He will probably use paper and pencil.

$$
\begin{array}{rcl}
4\frac{3}{4} & = & 4\frac{6}{8} \\
+ \ 2\frac{7}{8} & = & + \ 2\frac{7}{8} \\
\hline
& & 6\frac{13}{8} = 7\frac{5}{8} \text{ feet}
\end{array}
$$

Name _____ Date _____

1. Show how Alvin could have solved his problem with paper and pencil instead of a calculator. Discuss which method you prefer and why.

_____

_____

_____

_____

2. Show how Mr. Lee could have solved his problem using a calculator. Discuss why this answer is different from what Mr. Lee found.

_____

_____

_____

_____

Practice

Identify whether you would most likely use paper and pencil, a calculator, or mental computation to compute.

1. Find the change from $1.00. _____

2. Find the total weight of two items that weigh 9.85 ounces and 14.38 ounces. _____

3. Find the tip for a hair stylist. _____

4. Find the average price of a certain type of camera at 8 different stores. _____

Use two different methods to compute. Identify the most efficient method.

5. The length of each piece if a board that is $16\frac{1}{2}$ feet long is cut into 2 equal pieces.

6. The total cost if 38 people each bought a ticket for $28.25.

Part I Review

Vocabulary

Choose the letter of the word(s) that completes the sentence.

1. The answer to a subtraction problem is a _____.

   a. quotient   **b.** product   **c.** difference

2. The middle number when a group of numbers is arranged in order from least to greatest is called the _____.

   a. mean   **b.** median   **c.** mode

3. The number that you divide by in a division problem is called the _____.

   a. divisor   **b.** dividend   **c.** remainder

Skills

Add, subtract, multiply, or divide.

4. $1,999 + 860 + 374 =$ _____

5. $5.1 + 42.33 + 40.06 =$ _____

6. $374 + 5,063 + 993 =$ _____

7. $50,791 - 23,724 =$ _____

8. $87.6 - 18.39 =$ _____

9. $44.03 - 2.54 =$ _____

10. $5 \times 76 =$ _____

11. $3 \times 502 =$ _____

12. $8 \times 6.56 =$ _____

13. $9,035 \div 5 =$ _____

14. $792 \div 9 =$ _____

15. $0.84 \div 7 =$ _____

Rename as a percent.

16. $\frac{9}{100}$ _____

17. $\frac{700}{100}$ _____

18. $\frac{508}{100}$ _____

19. 0.71 _____

20. 0.02 _____

21. 0.068 _____

Rename as a decimal.

22. 76% _____

23. 5.9% _____

24. 900% _____

Find the answer.

25. 80% of 55 _____

26. $37\frac{1}{2}\%$ of 72 _____

27. 90% of 500 _____

Name _____ Date _____

Use a calculator to compute.

28. $7{,}912 + 1{,}136 + 705 =$ _____

29. $81.26 \times 62.81 =$ _____

30. $3 + 52.11 - 48.251 =$ _____

31. $50.5 \times 84.5 \div 25 =$ _____

Compute mentally.

32. $683 + 599 =$ _____

33. $10 \times 1.2 =$ _____

34. $599 \div 100 =$ _____

35. $37{,}106 \div 1{,}000 =$ _____

Estimate.

36. $9{,}168 + 6{,}451 \approx$ _____

37. $47.12 - 7.268 \approx$ _____

38. $0.67 \times 0.43 \approx$ _____

39. $52 \times 95 \approx$ _____

40. $31 \div 6 \approx$ _____

41. $613.8 \div 5.87 \approx$ _____

Solve.

42. A store sold 386 video game systems in October. In November, the store sold 431 video game systems, and in December, 621 video game systems. What was the total number of video game systems that the store sold during these 3 months? _____

43. A school band needs to save $8,600 for a trip. The band members have already saved $4,736. How much more do they need to save for the trip? _____

44. A chef had 29.4 pounds of chicken. She used 8.7 pounds of chicken during lunch. About how many pounds of chicken is left? _____

45. Goldfish cost $2.95 each. About how many goldfish can be purchased for $28? _____

Part I Test

Add, subtract, multiply, or divide.

1. 1,365
      + 4,713

2.   8.9
      + 68.3

3.   49.3
         0.12
      + 6.98

4. 7,639
      − 5,256

5.   53.9
      − 12.16

6.   80.09
      − 43.62

7. 106
      ×   3

8.   8.2
      ×   5

9. 9.05
      ×   3

10. 6)$\overline{5,796}$

11. 9)$\overline{45.9}$

12. 3)$\overline{7.92}$

Divide and round to the nearest hundredth.

13. 3)$\overline{6.19}$

14. 8)$\overline{2.45}$

15. 7)$\overline{8.01}$

Rename as a percent.

16. 34 per 100 _____

17. 0.059 _____

18. $\frac{3}{8}$ _____

19. $1\frac{1}{4}$ _____

20. 1.325 _____

21. 0.7 _____

Rename as a decimal and as a fraction.

22. 4.3% ⟶ decimal _____ ⟶ fraction _____

23. 90% ⟶ decimal _____ ⟶ fraction _____

24. 180% ⟶ decimal _____ ⟶ fraction _____

Use the following numbers to answer questions 25–27.

48, 45, 40, 48, 41

25. Find the mean: _____

26. Find the median: _____

27. Find the mode: _____

Name _____   Date _____

Use a calculator to compute.

28. $9,365 + 4,713 =$ _____   **29.** $49.3 + 0.12 + 6.98 =$ _____   **30.** $7,639 - 5,256 =$ _____

31. $80.09 - 43.62 =$ _____   **32.** $310.77 \div 1.35 =$ _____   **33.** $489.5 \times 48 \div 220 =$ _____

Use mental computation to add, subtract, multiply, or divide.

34. $786 + 110 =$ _____   **35.** $\$748 + \$690 =$ _____   **36.** $1.4 + 2.8 =$ _____

37. $64 - 49 =$ _____   **38.** $\$8.00 - \$5.99 =$ _____   **39.** $100 \times 56 =$ _____

40. $32.7 \div 10 =$ _____   **41.** $0.578 \times 1,000 =$ _____   **42.** $62.81 \div 10 =$ _____

Estimate.

43. $138 + 329 \approx$ _____   **44.** $587 - 321 \approx$ _____   **45.** $\$7.19 + \$3.85 \approx$ _____

46. $5.68 - 4.18 \approx$ _____   **47.** $95 \times 31 \approx$ _____   **48.** $85.1 \div 3.2 \approx$ _____

Estimate to choose the reasonable answer.

49. $59 + 37.2 + 598.7 \approx$ _____   **a.** 69.49   **b.** 694.9   **c.** 6,949

50. $8,190 \div 25 \approx$ _____   **a.** 3.276   **b.** 32.76   **c.** 327.6

Solve.

51. Muffins cost $2.25 and scones cost $1.85. What is the total cost for six muffins and four scones?

_____

52. The total cost of lunch for four people is $28.68. How much is each person's equal share of the cost?

_____

53. On Friday, 19,782 people visited an amusement park. On Saturday, 27,305 people visited the amusement park. About how many people visited the amusement park on the two days?

_____

The Mathematics of Personal Finance and Investment, SV 9780547625683

Part II:
Personal Finance

Pre-Skills Test

Add or subtract.

1. $475 + $819 = _____

2. $631.18 + $47.52 = _____

3. $789.56 + $123.48 = _____

4. $827 − $351 = _____

5. $303.50 − $126.40 = _____

6. $838.51 − $629.48 = _____

7. $134,097 + $238,692 = _____

8. $256,240 + $109,378 = _____

9. $309,472 − $168,341 = _____

10. $260,480 − $48,396 = _____

Rename as a percent.

11. 0.78 _____

12. 0.06 _____

13. 0.1924 _____

14. 0.5379321 _____

15. 0.0824877 _____

16. 0.9106025 _____

Multiply.

17. $0.9 \times $146 = _____

18. $0.8 \times $150 = _____

19. $0.7 \times $436 = _____

20. $0.85 \times $936 = _____

21. $0.73 \times $816 = _____

22. $0.62 \times $735 = _____

Name _____   Date _____

Estimate.

23. $6,400 ÷ 3 = _____

24. $19,201 ÷ 5 = _____

25. $37,200 ÷ 4 = _____

26. $197,600 ÷ 4 = _____

27. $41,830 ÷ 5 = _____

28. $76,921 ÷ 4 = _____

Divide. Round to the nearest dollar.

29. $316 ÷ 7 = _____

30. $407 ÷ 3 = _____

31. $723 ÷ 8 = _____

32. $573 ÷ 4 = _____

33. $825 ÷ 7 = _____

34. $999 ÷ 8 = _____

35. $1,200 ÷ 6 = _____

36. $2,600 ÷ 6 = _____

37. $5,100 ÷ 6 = _____

38. $7,800 ÷ 12 = _____

39. $9,400 ÷ 12 = _____

40. $16,000 ÷ 12 = _____

The Mathematics of Personal Finance and Investment, SV 9780547625683

Sales Tax

The most common form of tax we pay is the **sales tax**. Sales tax is computed as a percent of the total sales of goods and services.

The money raised from the sales tax is a major source of income for many state and local governments. The sales tax rate varies from state to state and from city to city.

Example 1: How much sales tax will you pay on a $10.80 book if the sales tax rate is $7\frac{1}{2}\%$?

$7\frac{1}{2}\%$ Sales Tax Table

Amount of Sales Tax			Amount of Sales Tax			Amount of Sales Tax		
0.01–	0.06	0.00	8.40–	8.73	0.65	17.27–	17.30	1.30
.07–	.19	.01	8.74–	8.86	.66	17.40–	17.63	1.31
.28–	.33	.02	8.87–	8.97	.67	17.54–	17.66	1.32
.34–	.46	.03	9.00–	9.13	.68	17.67–	17.79	1.33
.47–	.53	.04	9.14–	9.26	.69	17.80–	17.93	1.34
.60–	.73	.05	9.27–	9.39	.70	17.94–	18.06	1.35
.74–	.85	.06	9.40–	9.53	.71	18.07–	18.19	1.36
.87–	.90	.07	9.54–	9.66	.72	18.20–	18.33	1.37
1.00–	1.13	.08	9.67–	9.79	.73	18.34–	18.46	1.38
1.14–	1.26	.09	9.80–	9.93	.74	18.47–	18.59	1.39
1.27–	1.30	.10	9.94–	10.06	.75	18.60–	18.73	1.40
1.40–	1.53	.11	10.07–	10.19	.76	18.74–	18.86	1.41
1.54–	1.66	.12	10.20–	10.33	.77	18.87–	18.99	1.42
1.67–	1.79	.13	10.34–	10.46	.78	19.00–	19.13	1.43
1.80–	1.93	.14	10.47–	10.59	.79	19.14–	19.26	1.44
1.94–	2.06	.15	10.60–	10.73	.80	19.27–	19.39	1.45
2.07–	2.19	.16	(10.74–	10.86	.81)	19.40–	19.53	1.46
2.20–	2.33	.17	10.87–	10.99	.82	19.54–	19.66	1.47

Method 1: Use the partial table.
Since $10.80 is between $10.74 and $10.86, the sales tax will be $0.81.

Method 2: Multiply to find the tax.

THINK: $7\frac{1}{2}\% = 0.075$

$0.075 \times \$10.80 = \$0.81$

The sales tax will be $0.81.

Example 2: About how much sales tax will you pay on a purchase of $42.75 worth of CDs if the sales tax rate is 6%?

| Step 1 | Estimate 1% of $42.75.

THINK: $1\% = \frac{1}{100}$

$\frac{1}{100}$ of $42.75 = $42.75 \div 100$

$= \$0.4275$, or about $0.43

| Step 2 | Estimate 6% of $42.75.

Multiply mentally:
6% of $42.75 is about 6 × $0.43, or $2.58

The sales tax will be about $2.58.

Example 3: If the sales tax rate is 4%, what is the total cost of a pair of shoes priced at $39.50?

Method 1: Find the sales tax first.

| Step 1 | Multiply to find the sales tax.
THINK: 4% = 0.04

0.04 × $39.50 = $1.58

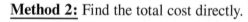

| Step 2 | Add to find the total cost.

$39.50 + $1.58 = $41.08

Method 2: Find the total cost directly.

THINK: Adding 4% makes the total cost 104% of the original price.
THINK: 104% = 1.04

Multiply to find the total cost.
1.04 × $39.50 = $41.08

The total cost of the shoes will be $41.08.

| **Think About It** |

Some people travel to other states or cities to do their shopping. Why do you think they do this? What hidden expenses are involved?

_____

_____

_____

_____

Practice

Remember to estimate whenever you use your calculator.
Use the partial sales tax table on page 39 to find the $7\frac{1}{2}\%$ sales tax on the purchase price.

1. $2.22 _____

2. $18.32 _____

3. $10.85 _____

4. $17.75 _____

5. $1.95 _____

6. $19.10 _____

Find the sales tax to the nearest cent.

Purchase price	Sales tax rate	Sales tax
$23.50	5%	**7.** _____
$98.99	6%	**8.** _____
$375.00	7%	**9.** _____
$165.95	$4\frac{1}{2}\%$	**10.** _____
$46.85	$5\frac{1}{2}\%$	**11.** _____
$3,575.00	$8\frac{1}{4}\%$	**12.** _____

Complete the table to find the estimated sales tax and exact sales tax. Round each amount to the nearest cent.

Purchase price	Sales tax rate	Estimated sales tax	Exact sales tax
$21.30	6%	**13.** _____	**14.** _____
$31.80	7%	**15.** _____	**16.** _____
$80.98	8%	**17.** _____	**18.** _____

The Mathematics of Personal Finance and Investment, SV 9780547625683

Name _____ Date _____

Complete the table to find the sales tax and total cost. Round each amount to the nearest cent.

Purchase price	Sales tax rate	Sales tax	Total cost
$17.50	5%	19. _____	20. _____
$85.99	$4\frac{1}{2}\%$	21. _____	22. _____
$257.00	6%	23. _____	24. _____
$4,786.50	$8\frac{1}{4}\%$	25. _____	26. _____
$10,162.75	$7\frac{1}{2}\%$	27. _____	28. _____

Solve. Round each amount to the nearest cent.

29. Karina buys a bicycle priced at $159.95. The sales tax rate is 8%.

    a. How much sales tax does Karina pay? _____

    b. What is the total cost of the bicycle? _____

30. Clayton buys a video game priced at $34.99. The sales tax rate is $7\frac{1}{4}\%$.

    a. How much sales tax does Clayton pay? _____

    b. What is the total cost of the video game? _____

31. Robert buys 3 T-shirts priced at $8.00 each. The sales tax rate is 6%.

    a. How much sales tax does Robert pay? _____

    b. What is the total cost of the T-shirts? _____

32. An office manager buys a computer priced at $750 and a monitor priced at $164. The sales tax rate is 7%.

    a. How much sales tax does the manager pay? _____

    b. What is the total cost of the items? _____

33. Hester wants to buy a sofa priced at $820.

    a. In Hester's city, the sales tax rate is $8\frac{1}{4}\%$. How much will she pay in sales tax in her city? _____

    b. In a neighboring city, the sales tax rate is $6\frac{1}{2}\%$. How much will Hester pay in sales tax in the neighboring city? _____

    c. How much will Hester save in sales tax if she buys the sofa in the neighboring city? _____

Name _____   Date _____

Purchasing Power

It seems that you pay more for things each year. In fact, most prices have risen steadily during the past decades. The **Consumer Price Index (CPI)** is a number that represents the value of a variety of goods and services bought by a typical city family. The Consumer Price Index has gone up over 150% since 1980.

This steady increase in prices is called **inflation**. The **inflation rate** is the percent that prices increase over time.

Example 1: Suppose that in January, the average cost of food for your family was $143 per week. At the end of the year, the average cost of food was $159 per week. What was the inflation rate for your food costs? Round to the nearest tenth of a percent.

> Inflation Rate = Price Increase ÷ Original Price

Step 1 Subtract to find the price increase.

$159 − $143 = $16

Step 2 Divide to find the inflation rate.

$16 ÷ $143 ≈ 0.1118

Step 3 Rename as a percent.

11.2%

The inflation rate was about 11.2%

The Mathematics of Personal Finance and Investment, SV 9780547625683

As the inflation rate goes up, the purchasing power goes down. The **purchasing power** of a dollar is how much a dollar will buy.

Example 2: Neil's income is $27,000 per year. During the year, the inflation rate was 4%. What was the purchasing power of Neil's income after inflation?

| Step 1 | Multiply to find the decrease in purchasing power.
THINK: 4% = 0.04

0.04 × $27,000 = $1,080

| Step 2 | Subtract to find the purchasing power after inflation.

$27,000 − $1,080 = $25,920

Neil's $27,000 salary had the purchasing power of $25,920 after inflation.

Think About It

1. How could you be sure that your income was keeping up with inflation?

_____

_____

_____

2. If a person has a fixed income, their income does not change from one year to the next. Why is inflation especially difficult for people with fixed incomes?

_____

_____

_____

Practice

Remember to estimate whenever you use your calculator.

Complete the tables to find the inflation rates to the nearest tenth of a percent.

Item	Sports tickets	Weekly food	Monthly rent
Current price	$30.00	$183.00	$650
Original price	$26.00	$167.00	$625
Price increase	1. _____	2. _____	3. _____
Inflation rate	4. _____	5. _____	6. _____

Item	Car rental	Gallon of gasoline	Jeans
Current price	$104.00	$3.15	$33.89
Original price	$89.00	$2.74	$31.95
Price increase	7. _____	8. _____	9. _____
Inflation rate	10. _____	11. _____	12. _____

Complete the table to find the purchasing power after inflation. Round each amount to the nearest cent.

Net income	Inflation rate	Decrease in purchasing power	Purchasing power after inflation
$22,500	3%	13. _____	14. _____
$24,600	4%	15. _____	16. _____
$28,750	2%	17. _____	18. _____
$30,325	1.5%	19. _____	20. _____
$34,875	3.5%	21. _____	22. _____
$42,200	0.5%	23. _____	24. _____

Name _____ Date _____

Solve.

25. Originally, a box of your favorite cereal cost $2.89. Now the price is $3.29.

   a. By how much did the price increase? _____

   b. What was the inflation rate to the nearest tenth of a percent? _____

26. Last month, a box of paper clips cost $1.89. This month, the price is $1.95.

   a. By how much did the price increase? _____

   b. What was the inflation rate to the nearest tenth of a percent? _____

27. The original subscription price for a magazine was $19.95 per year. The price was raised to $22.95 per year.

   a. By how much did the price increase? _____

   b. What was the inflation rate to the nearest tenth of a percent? _____

28. Andy's income is $26,400. During the past year, the inflation rate was 2.5%. What was the purchasing power of his income after inflation? _____

> **Extension**   **Deflation**

A steady decrease in prices is called **deflation**. The prices of some goods and services have deflated during the past decades.

Example: Originally, a certain laptop computer cost $665. Now it costs $530. What was the rate of deflation? Round to the nearest tenth of a percent.

| **Step 1** | Subtract to find the price decrease. |

     $665 − $530 = $135

| **Step 2** | Divide to find the deflation rate. |

     $135 ÷ $665 ≈ 0.2030

     The deflation rate was about 20.3%

Find the deflation rate to the nearest tenth of a percent.

  1. Current price: $350
     Original price: $420 _____

  2. Current price: $1,165
     Original price: $1,830 _____

  3. Current price: $0.99
     Original price: $1.29 _____

  4. Current price: $20.50
     Original price: $22.50 _____

Fixed and Variable Expenses

You are working on a monthly budget. A **budget** is an organized plan for spending money. Your monthly budget has three types of expenses:

> **Fixed money expenses,** which are the same each month.
>
> **Living expenses,** which vary from month to month.
>
> **Annual expenses,** which are amounts to be paid each year.

Fixed expenses include rent and car payments. When you budget fixed expenses, you use the actual amount of the expense.

Living expenses include food, utilities, and transportation. When you budget living expenses, you use an average, or mean, of past expenses.

Example 1: In the last 3 months, your family spent $116, $76, and $136 for transportation. How much should you budget next month for transportation? Round to the nearest dollar.

| Step 1 | Add to find the total of past expenses.

$116 + $76 + $136 = $328

| Step 2 | Divide to find the average expenses.

$328 ÷ 3 ≈ $109.33

You should budget $109 next month for transportation.

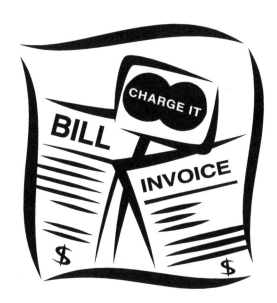

Annual expenses include insurance premiums, medical bills, and vacations. To budget the monthly share of annual expenses, divide the annual expense by 12.

Example 2: Francisco plans to spend $1,000 per year on vacations. How much should he budget as the monthly share of the vacation expenses? Round to the nearest dollar.

Divide the annual expense by 12.
$1,000 \div 12 \approx \$83.33$

Francisco should budget $83 as the monthly share of vacation expenses.

| Think About It |

1. How could you predict monthly changes in some living expenses?

_____

_____

_____

2. What problems might arise from budgeting part of an annual expense each month? How could these problems be avoided?

_____

_____

_____

Practice

Remember to estimate whenever you use your calculator.
Complete the table to find the amounts to be budgeted for April. Round to the nearest dollar.

Living expense	January	February	March	Amount budgeted for April
Food	$378	$472	$434	1. _____
Utilities	$178	$105	$116	2. _____
Clothing	$67	$83	$105	3. _____
Entertainment	$58	$46	$63	4. _____

Name _____ Date _____

Complete the table to find the amount to be budgeted for April. Round to the nearest dollar.

Living expense	January	February	March	Amount budgeted for April
Home phone	$22	$26	$19	5. _____
Cell phone	$72	$96	$84	6. _____
Personal expenses	$76	$92	$126	7. _____
Contributions	$13	$15	$18	8. _____
Laundry	$20	$23	$15	9. _____
Car care	$62	$50	$80	10. _____
Eating out	$160	$107	$192	11. _____
Books and magazines	$55	$29	$34	12. _____

Find the monthly share of the annual expense. Round to the nearest dollar.

13. Vacation: $1,200 _____

14. Medical: $450 _____

15. Car insurance: $1,050 _____

16. Life insurance: $315 _____

17. Car repairs: $685 _____

18. Health insurance: $1,260 _____

Solve. Round to the nearest dollar.

19. Dave spent $45, $18, and $51 over the past 3 months on entertainment. How much should he budget next month for entertainment? _____

20. The Monahans spent $467, $521, and $428 over the past 3 months on food. How much should they budget next month for food? _____

The Mathematics of Personal Finance and Investment, SV 9780547625683

Name _____ Date _____

Solve. Round to the nearest dollar.

21. Celia spent $300, $425, $295, and $375 over the past 4 months on transportation. How much should she budget next month for transportation?

_____

22. Carlos expects to spend $1,100 this year on home repairs. How much should he budget as the monthly share? _____

23. The Brancas spent $92, $79, and $87 on clothing over the last 3 months. How much should they budget next month for clothing? _____

24. Martin expects to spend $89 this year on car registration and license fees. How much should he budget as the monthly share? _____

25. Shelia spent $89, $93, and $88 over the last 3 months on utilities. How much should she budget next month for utilities? _____

26. Margo expects to spend $840 this year on car repairs. How much should she budget as the monthly share? _____

27. The Runningbears expect to spend $5,500 this year on medical expenses. How much should they budget as the monthly share? _____

28. Betty spent $46, $54, $68, $50, and $42 on her electricity bill over the past 5 months. How much should she budget for electricity next month?

_____

29. The Grabowskis spent $85, $96, $108, and $99 on books and magazines during the past 4 months. How much should they budget for books and magazines next month? _____

30. During the past 6 months, the Fields spent the following amounts on cell phone expenses: $65, $85, $75, $60, $70, and $90. How much should they budget for cell phone expenses next month?

_____

Name _____ Date _____

Budgeting Expenses

You can use a **budget sheet** to plan how much to spend each month. You add the living expenses, fixed expenses, and monthly shares of annual expenses to find the total budget. You need to make sure that your total monthly budget does not exceed your monthly income.

Example: Read this budget sheet for Carl and Gloria Delcor.

BUDGET SHEET FOR THE MONTH OF *March*
FOR *Carl & Gloria Delcor*

LIVING EXPENSES		FIXED EXPENSES	
Food	$453	Rent	$650
HOUSEHOLD		Mortgage	
Electricity	$76	Car Payment	$225
Natural Gas	$34	Savings	$40
Telephone	$18	Contingency	$30
Cell Phone	$42	**TOTAL**	
Cable/Internet	$83	**ANNUAL EXPENSES**	
Water			
Other _____		**INSURANCE**	
		Life	$105
TRANSPORTATION		Home	$224
Gas/Oil	$94	Car	$780
Parking/Tolls	$15	Medical/Dental	$1,683
Repairs	$85	Vacation	$700
Bus/Train/Cab	$5	Property Taxes	
Other _____		Home Repairs	
		TOTAL	
PERSONAL		**MONTHLY SHARE**	
Clothing	$46	**MONTHLY SUMMARY**	
Expenses	$75		
Credit Card		**NET INCOME**	
ENTERTAINMENT		**TOTALS**	
Movies/Sports	$18	Living	
Eating Out	$47	Fixed	
TOTAL		Annual	
(LIVING EXPENSES)		**TOTAL EXPENSES**	
		BALANCE	

These amounts may vary seasonally.

Use what you know about changing prices to budget this amount.

Add to find the total living expenses.

Savings are considered a fixed expense.

The contingency fund is for unexpected expenses.

List the annual amounts.

Divide the TOTAL by 12 to find the MONTHLY SHARE.

NET INCOME is take-home pay.

BALANCE = NET INCOME – TOTAL EXPENSES

The Mathematics of Personal Finance and Investment, SV 9780547625683

Name _____ Date _____

Think About It

1. What could you do if your monthly expenses were more than your monthly income?

   _____

   _____

2. How would the budget for a single person be different from the budget for a family?

   _____

   _____

   _____

Practice

Remember to estimate whenever you use a calculator.
Use the budget sheet on page 51 to solve.

1. How much was budgeted for gas and oil?

   _____

2. How much was budgeted for a car payment?

   _____

3. How much was budgeted for car insurance?

   _____

4. Find the total monthly budget for living expenses.

   _____

5. Find the total monthly budget for fixed expenses.

   _____

6. Find the total budget for annual expenses.

   _____

7. Find the monthly share of annual expenses.

   _____

8. Find the total monthly budget for all expenses.

   _____

9. Carl and Gloria Delcor have a combined monthly net income of $2,510. What is their balance for this monthly budget? _____

10. Suppose Carl and Gloria's net income were to drop to $2,319. How much more would they need to earn per month for the balance to be 0? _____

Name _____   Date _____

Use the budget sheet on page 51 to solve.

11. Suppose Carl and Gloria's annual medical/dental costs increased to $4,827.

   a. Find the total budget for annual expenses.

   _____

   b. Find the monthly share of annual expenses.

   _____

   c. How much more than their $2,510 monthly income would they need to earn to have a balance of 0? _____

12. Suppose Carl and Gloria bought a house and their mortgage payment was $712 per month. Water costs $22 per month and property taxes were $2,400 per year. Homeowner's insurance went up to $356. They stopped paying rent, and all other expenses were the same.

   a. Find the total monthly budget for living expenses.

   _____

   b. Find the total monthly budget for fixed expenses.

   _____

   c. Find the monthly share of annual expenses.

   _____

   d. Find the total monthly budget for all expenses.

   _____

   e. How much extra income do Carl and Gloria need per month? _____

13. Suppose Carl and Gloria had a credit card balance of $1,800. They budgeted to pay off 10% of the remaining balance each month.

   a. How much will they pay the 1st month?

   _____

   b. How much will they pay the 2nd month? (Remember: After each month's payment, the remaining balance decreases.) _____

   c. How much would they still owe after 2 months?

   _____

Name _____ Date _____

Use the budget sheet to solve.

14. How much was budgeted for cable/Internet? _____

15. How much was budgeted for home insurance? _____

16. Find the total monthly budget for living expenses. _____

17. Find the total monthly budget for fixed expenses. _____

18. Find the total budget for annual expenses. _____

19. Find the monthly share of annual expenses. _____

20. Find the total monthly budget for all expenses. _____

21. Ann and Joe Furillo have a combined monthly net income of $3,090. What is their balance for this monthly budget? _____

22. Suppose Ann and Joe bought a new car, and the monthly payment was $435. Their new car insurance was $1,294 per year.

    a. Find the new fixed expenses. _____

    b. Find the new monthly share of annual expenses. _____

    c. Find the new total monthly expenses. _____

    d. How much more than their $3,090 monthly income would they need to earn to have a balance of 0? _____

BUDGET SHEET FOR THE MONTH OF April FOR Ann and Joe Furillo			
LIVING EXPENSES		**FIXED EXPENSES**	
Food	$492	Rent	
HOUSEHOLD		Mortgage	$804
Electricity	$84	Car Payment	
Natural Gas	$36	Savings	$35
Telephone	$20	Contingency	$35
Cell Phone	$65	**TOTAL**	
Cable/Internet	$61	**ANNUAL EXPENSES**	
Water	$15		
Other _____	_____	**INSURANCE**	
		Life	$105
TRANSPORTATION		Home	$325
Gas/Oil	$112	Car	$850
Parking/Tolls	$22	Medical/Dental	$1,800
Repairs	$72	Vacation	$500
Bus/Train/Cab		Property Taxes	$2,650
Other _____	_____	Home Repairs	$250
PERSONAL		**TOTAL**	
Clothing	$104	**MONTHLY SHARE**	
Expenses	$70	**MONTHLY SUMMARY**	
Credit Card		**NET INCOME**	
ENTERTAINMENT		**TOTALS**	
Movies/Sports	$24	Living	
Eating Out	$36	Fixed	
TOTAL		Annual	
(LIVING EXPENSES)		**TOTAL EXPENSES**	
		BALANCE	

The Mathematics of Personal Finance and Investment, SV 9780547625683

Name _____ Date _____

Problem Solving Application: Budgeting

Recall that a budget is a plan for using money. The Williams family decided to control their expenses by making and following a budget. This circle graph shows how they decided to allot their family income after taxes.

Use the circle graph to answer problems 1–12.

What part of the budget is allotted to:

1. housing? _____

2. food? _____

3. clothing? _____

4. savings? _____

Is more money allotted to:

5. transportation or clothing? _____

6. entertainment or medical care? _____

7. food or clothing? _____

8. savings or entertainment? _____

9. For which type of expense did they allot the greatest part of their budget? _____

Which expense represents:

10. $\frac{40}{100}$ of the budget? _____

11. 4% of the budget? _____

12. 0.15 of the budget? _____

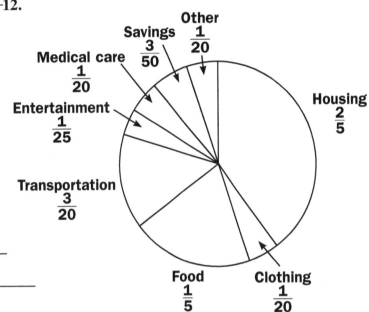

The Williams' Budget

Name _____ Date _____

This circle graph shows the Henderson family's budget.

Use the circle graph to answer problems 13–30.

What part of the budget is allotted to:

13. transportation? _____

14. mortgage? _____

15. clothing? _____

16. health insurance? _____

17. homeowners insurance? _____

18. food? _____

19. entertainment? _____

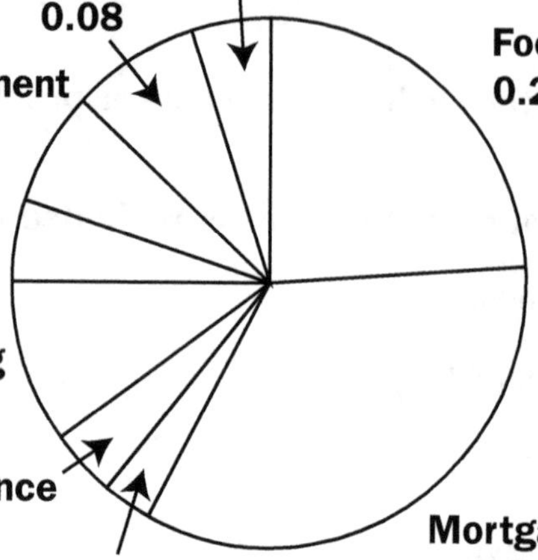

Is more money allotted to:

20. entertainment or transportation? _____

21. mortgage or food? _____

22. transportation or savings? _____

23. health insurance or homeowners insurance? _____

24. savings or clothing? _____

25. For which type of expense is the smallest part of the budget allotted? _____

Which expense represents:

26. $\frac{24}{100}$ of the budget? _____

27. $\frac{4}{100}$ of the budget? _____

28. $\frac{1}{10}$ of the budget? _____

29. 34% of the budget? _____

30. 7% of the budget? _____

The Hendersons' Budget

Savings 0.08
Transportation 0.05
Entertainment 0.07
Food 0.24
Other 0.05
Clothing 0.10
Health insurance 0.04
Homeowners insurance 0.03
Mortgage 0.34

The Mathematics of Personal Finance and Investment, SV 9780547625683

Name _____ Date _____

This circle graph shows the Dyer family's budget.

Use the circle graph to answer problems 31–48.

What part of the budget is allotted to:

31. personal? _____

32. car payment? _____

33. savings? _____

34. vacation? _____

35. food? _____

36. transportation? _____

37. insurance? _____

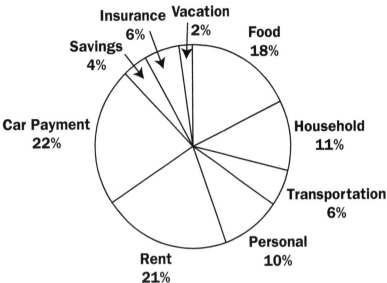

The Dyers' Budget

Insurance 6% · Vacation 2% · Savings 4% · Food 18% · Car Payment 22% · Household 11% · Transportation 6% · Personal 10% · Rent 21%

Is more money allotted to:

38. food or car payment? _____

39. transportation or savings? _____

40. household or personal? _____

41. food or rent? _____

42. savings or vacation? _____

43. For which type of expense is the greatest part of the budget allotted? _____

Which expense represents:

44. 0.22 of the budget? _____

45. 0.02 of the budget? _____

46. $\frac{18}{100}$ of the budget? _____

47. $\frac{1}{10}$ of the budget? _____

48. $\frac{1}{25}$ of the budget? _____

Name _____ Date _____

The Bartner family made a budget. They allotted their income as follows: food, 0.16; housing 0.30; clothing, 0.06; savings, 0.125; transportation, 0.20; entertainment, 0.05; medical care, 0.05; other, 0.055. **Use this information to answer problems 49–51.**

49. For which types of expense did they allot more than 0.15 of their budget?

_____

_____

50. Rewrite the Bartners' budget using fractions in simplest form.

Food _____   Housing _____

Clothing _____   Savings _____

Transportation _____   Entertainment _____

Medical care _____   Other _____

51. Suppose you wanted to arrange the Bartner budget items in order from greatest to least. Do you think it would be easier to use decimals or fractions? Why?

_____

_____

The Liu family made a budget. They allotted their income as follows: food, $\frac{3}{20}$; housing $\frac{8}{25}$; clothing, $\frac{9}{100}$; savings, $\frac{7}{50}$; transportation, $\frac{7}{100}$; entertainment, $\frac{2}{25}$; medical care, $\frac{9}{100}$; other, $\frac{3}{50}$. **Use this information to answer problems 52–54.**

52. Rewrite the Liu's budget using percents.

Food _____   Transportation _____

Housing _____   Entertainment _____

Clothing _____   Medical care _____

Savings _____   Other _____

53. For which types of expense did they allot more than $\frac{1}{10}$ of their budget?

_____

_____

54. Arrange the Liu's budget items in order from greatest to least.

_____

_____

The Cost of Raising a Family

When you raise a family, you need to plan now for expenses you will have later. Raising children will be one of your biggest expenses.

According to some experts, it will cost about $45,340 to raise a child born today until he or she reaches age 5.

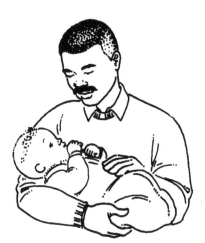

Example 1: Lisa and Gary just had a baby named Nicole. About how much will the average yearly cost be to raise Nicole until she is age 5?

Step 1 Divide.

$45,340 \div 5 = \$9,068$

Step 2 Round to the nearest $1,000.

$9,068 rounds to $9,000.

It will cost about $9,000 per year to raise Nicole until she is age 5.

These same experts think that it will cost about $160,620 to raise that child from age 5 to age 18.

Example 2: About how much will the average yearly cost be for Lisa and Gary to raise Nicole from age 5 until she is age 18?

THINK: There are 13 years from the 5th birthday to the 18th birthday.

Step 1 Divide.

$160,620 \div 13 \approx \$12,355.38$

Step 2 Round to the nearest $1,000.

$12,355.38 rounds to $12,000.

It will cost about $12,000 per year to raise Nicole from age 5 to age 18.

When Nicole is 18, it could cost $283,100 to pay her tuition and fees for 4 years at a private college or $78,900 for 4 years at a public college.

Example 3: About how much would Nicole's tuition and fees be each year?

Divide to find the annual tuition. Then round to the nearest $1,000.

Private college

$283,100 ÷ 4 = $70,775

$70,775 rounds to $71,000.

Public college

$78,900 ÷ 4 = $19,725

$19,725 rounds to $20,000.

Tuition and fees would be about $71,000 per year for private college and $20,000 per year for public college.

Raising a family can be expensive.

Example 4: About how much would it cost Lisa and Gary to raise Nicole through age 18 and pay her tuition and fees for 4 years at a private college?

Add. Then round to the nearest $1,000.

$45,340 + $160,620 + $283,100 = $489,060
$489,060 rounds to $489,000.

It would cost Lisa and Gary about $489,000.

Think About It

1. How does inflation affect the amount it costs to raise a child and pay for college tuition?

_____

_____

2. What steps could a person take to prepare for the costs of raising a family?

_____

_____

Practice

Remember to estimate whenever you use your calculator.
Use the table below for problems 1–20.

ESTIMATED COSTS OF RAISING A FAMILY

Child born	Birth to 5 years	Ages 5 to 18	4-year private college	4-year public college
Last year	$44,110	$156,260	$269,620	$75,130
This year	$45,340	$160,620	$283,100	$78,900
Next year	$46,610	$165,100	$297,260	$82,830
2 years from now	$47,910	$169,710	$312,120	$86,970
3 years from now	$49,240	$174,440	$327,730	$91,320

Complete the table to find the average yearly costs. Round each to the nearest $1,000.

Child born	Birth to 5 years	Ages 5 to 18	Private college	Public college
Last year	1. _____	2. _____	3. _____	4. _____
Next year	5. _____	6. _____	7. _____	8. _____
2 years from now	9. _____	10. _____	11. _____	12. _____
3 years from now	13. _____	14. _____	15. _____	16. _____

Solve.

17. A child will be born next year. About how much will it cost to raise the child to age 18?

    _____

18. About how much will it cost to raise a child born last year from age 5 to age 18 and pay 4 years of public college tuition? _____

19. About how much will it cost to raise a child who will be born 2 years from now and pay 4 years of tuition for a private college? _____

20. About how much will it cost to raise a child who will be born 3 years from now and pay 4 years of tuition for a private college? _____

Name _____ Date _____

Use the information in the table on page 61 for problems 21–30.

21. About how much will it cost to raise a child born last year to age 18? _____

22. About how much will it cost to raise a child born this year to age 18? _____

23. About how much will it cost to raise a child born last year from birth to age 18 and pay 4 years of private college tuition? _____

24. About how much will it cost to raise a child born this year from age 5 to age 18 and pay 4 years of public college tuition? _____

25. About how much will it cost to raise a child born next year to age 18 and pay 4 years of tuition for a public college? _____

26. About how much will it cost to raise a child who will be born 2 years from now to age 18?

   _____

27. About how much will it cost to raise a child who will be born 3 years from now and pay 4 years of tuition for a public college? _____

28. About how much more expensive will it be to raise a child and pay 4 years of private college tuition if the child is born 2 years from now and not this year?

   _____

29. About how much less expensive will it be to pay 4 years of public college tuition instead of private college tuition for a child who will be born 3 years from now? _____

30. About how much more expensive will it be to pay 4 years of tuition for a private college instead of a public college for a child who will be born next year? _____

Determining Net Worth

Maria and Roberto are trying to determine their net worth. They got out records that showed all they owned (**assets**) and all they owed (**liabilities**). Their **net worth** is the difference between their assets and their liabilities.

Example 1: Maria and Roberto's assets are listed below. What is the total value of their assets?

THINK: Add to find the total value.

ASSETS	*Maria and Roberto Sanchez*
Checking and savings account(s)	$6,432
Cash	$312
Stocks and bonds	—
Retirement account(s)	$4,518
Car	$7,200
House	$153,000
Contents of house	$27,500
Collections, etc. *Baseball cards*	$489
TOTAL ASSETS	$199,451

Example 2: Maria and Roberto's liabilities are listed below. What is the total value of their liabilities?

THINK: Add to find the total value.

LIABILITIES	*Maria and Roberto Sanchez*
Balance on mortgage	$86,830
Balance on auto loan	$14,800
Balance on other loans	$2,630
Balance on credit cards	$890
TOTAL LIABILITIES	$105,150

Name _____ Date _____

To determine net worth, you subtract liabilities from assets.

Example 3: Find Maria and Roberto's net worth.

Subtract.
$199,451 − $105,150 = $94,301.

Maria and Roberto's net worth is $94,301.

Think About It

1. How would the net worth of a homeowner be different from the net worth of a renter?

_____

_____

2. Why is a person's net worth not a good indication of the amount of money he or she has available?

_____

_____

Practice

Remember to estimate whenever you use your calculator.
Use the assets and liabilities listed below for problems 1–3.

ASSETS	*Bill and Sally Jefferson*
Checking/savings/cash	$7,784
Stocks/bonds	$2,300
Retirement	$3,438
Car	$6,750
House	$167,800
Contents of house	$25,700
Collections, etc.	$1,864
TOTAL ASSETS	_____

LIABILITIES	*Bill and Sally Jefferson*
Balance on mortgage	$124,083
Balance on auto loan	$6,660
Balance on other loans	$8,700
Balance on credit cards	$4,526
TOTAL LIABILITIES	_____

1. How much do Bill and Sally have in checking, savings, and cash? _____

2. What is the balance on Bill and Sally's mortgage? _____

3. What is the total value of Bill and Sally's house and contents? _____

Name _____ Date _____

Use the assets and liabilities listed on page 64 for problems 4–17.

4. What is the value of Bill and Sally's car?

   _____

5. What is the balance on Bill and Sally's car loan?

   _____

6. What is the total of Bill and Sally's assets?

   _____

7. What is the total value of Bill and Sally's liabilities?

   _____

8. What is Bill and Sally's net worth? _____

Suppose Bill and Sally got a second mortgage of $45,000 to put an addition on their house. The addition caused the value of the house to increase by $47,600. The value of the house contents increased by $4,200. Their checking, savings, and cash dropped to $513. All their other assets and liabilities stayed the same.

9. What is the value of their house with the addition?

   _____

10. What is the new value of the contents of the house?

    _____

11. By how much did their checking, savings, and cash decrease? _____

12. What is the mortgage balance, including the second mortgage? _____

13. What is the new total of Bill and Sally's assets?

    _____

14. By how much did their total assets increase?

    _____

15. What is the new total of Bill and Sally's liabilities?

    _____

16. By how much did their total liabilities increase?

    _____

17. What is Bill and Sally's new net worth?

    _____

Name _____ Date _____

Use the assets and liabilities listed below for problems 18–28.

ASSETS	Anna and Chu Wong
Checking/savings/cash	$6,578
Stocks/bonds	—
Retirement	$3,375
Car	$8,540
House	$109,200
Contents of house	$23,670
Collections, etc.	$675
TOTAL ASSETS	_____

LIABILITIES	Anna and Chu Wong
Balance on mortgage	$63,477
Balance on auto loan	$2,034
Balance on other loans	$2,798
Balance on credit cards	$1,236
TOTAL LIABILITIES	_____

18. How much is in Anna and Chu's retirement account? _____

19. What is the balance on Anna and Chu's auto loan? _____

20. What is the balance on Anna and Chu's credit cards? _____

21. How much is Anna and Chu's car worth? _____

22. What is the total value of Anna and Chu's house and contents? _____

23. What is the total of Anna and Chu's assets? _____

24. What is the total of Anna and Chu's liabilities?_____

25. What is Anna and Chu's net worth? _____

Suppose Anna and Chu trade in their car for a new one. The value of their car is now $19,500, and the balance on their auto loan is now $13,994. All their other assets and liabilities remain the same as above.

26. What is the new total of Anna and Chu's assets? _____

27. What is the new total of Anna and Chu's liabilities? _____

28. What is Anna and Chu's new net worth? _____

Name _____ Date _____

Decision Making: Developing a Budget

Developing a budget for a club or organization requires group decisions, an understanding of the situation, and often compromise.

PROBLEM

The student officers of the Science Club are meeting to develop a budget for next year's activities. The budget must then be presented to the school's Funding Committee for approval.

Since money is limited, the budget must be done carefully and include complete explanations of how the funds will be used. The students think that they can probably get more than the $750 the club got last year.

Several of the 1,250 students in the school have submitted suggestions for what they would like to see done next year. The officers study each suggestion and estimate costs.

Suggested Activities
• Bus trip to the Science Museum for the Science Club members.   Charter bus: $250   Admission tickets: $6 each for 37 members
• Help students pay for supplies for their Science Fair projects.   About 40 students: $10 per student
• Sponsor a Health Fair at the school using volunteers from various health professions.   Publicity: $50   Decorations, displays: $50   Refreshments: $150
• Build a simple greenhouse for students interested in plant science.   Materials: $300
• Plant trees in front of the school.   Cost: 10 trees at about $30 each

DECISION-MAKING FACTORS

• Expense

• Benefits to student body

• Educational value

• Benefits to school

The Mathematics of Personal Finance and Investment, SV 9780547625683

DECISION-MAKING COMPARISONS

Complete the table. For "Expense," give a dollar amount. For "Educational value" and "Benefits to student body," write *Excellent, Good, Limited,* or *None.* For "Benefits to school," write *Yes* or *No.*

Item	Expense	Educational value	Benefits to student body	Benefits to school
Bus trip	1. _____	Excellent	2. _____	3. _____
Science Fair aid	4. _____	5. _____	Limited	6. _____
Health Fair	7. _____	8. _____	9. _____	Yes
Greenhouse	$300	10. _____	11. _____	12. _____
Trees	13. _____	14. _____	15. _____	16. _____

MAKING THE DECISIONS

Which items should be in the budget:

17. if the plan was to benefit the school?

_____

18. if the plan was to benefit the most students?

_____

19. if the plan was to provide the most educational value?

_____

20. What benefits could planting trees provide?

_____

21. What benefits could building a greenhouse provide?

_____

Select items for each type of budget, and make a circle graph to display the budget.

22. A budget that will most benefit all the students in the school.

23. A budget that will most benefit the school.

24. A budget that will most benefit the Science Club members.

Decision Making: Adjusting a Budget

A **balanced budget** has enough income to meet expenses. It is important to have a balanced budget. You cannot continue to spend more than you earn.

PROBLEM

The Nampo family has a decision to make. Their income is $512 less than their expenses. They listed these three plans to help them decide what to do.

PLAN A: The Nampos could try to bring home $512 more per month. They would need to earn about $640 to bring home an extra $512.

PLAN B: The Nampos could cut $512 from their budget. They would cut the $75 savings from fixed costs. The other cuts would have to come from living expenses.

PLAN C: The Nampos could try to bring home $260 more per month. They would need to earn about $328 to bring home an extra $260. They would cut the other $252 from the budget. They would make all their cuts from living expenses.

BUDGET SHEET FOR THE MONTH OF _April_ FOR _the Nampo Family_			
LIVING EXPENSES		**FIXED EXPENSES**	
Food	$669	Rent	—
HOUSEHOLD		Mortgage	$774
Electricity	$139	Car Payment	$180
Natural Gas	$61	Savings	$75
Telephone	$18	Contingency	$60
Cell Phone	$54	**TOTAL**	$1,089
Cable/Internet	$52	**ANNUAL EXPENSES**	
Water	$17	**INSURANCE**	
Other _____	—	Life	$215
TRANSPORTATION		Home	$462
Gas/Oil	$236	Car	$925
Parking/Tolls	—	Medical/Dental	$1,340
Repairs	$90	Vacation	$900
Bus/Train/Cab	$52	Property Taxes	$2,782
Other _____	—	Home Repairs	$168
PERSONAL		**TOTAL**	$6,792
Clothing	$135	**MONTHLY SHARE**	$566
Expenses	$225	**MONTHLY SUMMARY**	
Credit Card	—	**NET INCOME**	$3,167
ENTERTAINMENT		**TOTALS**	
Movies/Sports	$45	Living	$2,024
Eating Out	$231	Fixed	$1,089
TOTAL	$2,024	Annual	$566
(LIVING EXPENSES)		**TOTAL EXPENSES**	$3,679
		BALANCE	−$512

Name _____ Date _____

DECISION-MAKING FACTORS

- Living expenses
- Fixed expenses
- Total expenses
- Net income
- Balance
- Extra hours worked
- Other factors

DECISION-MAKING COMPARISONS

Compare the three plans by completing the table.

Factors	Plan A	Plan B	Plan C
Living expenses	$2,024	1. _____	2. _____
Fixed expenses	3. _____	4. _____	$1,089
Total expenses (including share of annual expenses)	5. _____	$3,167	6. _____
Net income	$3,679	7. _____	8. _____
Balance	9. _____	10. _____	0
Extra hours worked each month at $21/h	About 30.5 h	11. _____	12. _____
Other factors: Extra hours away from home per week	About 8 h	13. _____	14. _____

MAKING THE DECISIONS

Which plan should the Nampos choose if the only factor were:

15. Having a higher net salary? _____

16. Not reducing living costs? _____

17. Not working additional hours? _____

18. How much lower would the Nampos' living expenses be if they choose Plan C instead of Plan A?
_____

19. How would you advise the Nampos to cut living expenses if they choose Plan B?

_____

20. How would you advise the Nampos to cut living expenses if they choose Plan C?

_____

21. Which of these plans would you choose? Why?

_____

_____

Name _____   Date _____

Money Tips 1

Investing in collectibles may help you fight inflation and make a profit.

LET'S LOOK AT THE FACTS

Many people collect things, not simply as a hobby, but because certain things tend to increase in value over time. Following is a list of categories that could include **collectible items**.

1. Coins
2. Stamps
3. Fine art
4. Comic books
5. Autographs
6. Old flags
7. Film or television props
8. Rare books
9. Old vinyl records
10. Classic cars
11. Foreign currency
12. Ancient porcelain
13. Diamonds/gemstones
14. Historical photos
15. Original manuscripts
16. Items belonging to celebrities
17. Trading cards
18. Antique glassware

LET'S DISCUSS WHY

1. There is only one 1856 British Guiana 1-cent magenta stamp remaining in the world. In 1962, it was valued at $55,000. It was last sold in 1980 for $935,000. What was the percent of increase in the stamp's value from 1962 to 1980? _____

2. In 2000, a copy of a comic book that first introduced a famous superhero sold for $140,000. In 2011, this same copy sold for $1,100,000. What was the percent of increase in the comic book's value from 2000 to 2011? _____

3. A drawing done by a famous artist was certified authentic by an art expert. What else might make it even more valuable?

_____

_____

4. Why would some items increase in value while others would not?

_____

_____

_____

5. List some examples of collectible items for each of these categories. What do you think determines the value of each?

a. Film or television props

_____

_____

b. Historical photos

_____

_____

c. Original manuscripts

_____

_____

d. Items belonging to celebrities

_____

_____

LET'S SEE WHAT YOU WOULD DO

6. You inherit a large wooden box from your uncle. Inside is a collection of baseball cards, an autographed bat, three autographed baseballs, an old baseball glove, and several World Series ticket stubs. How would you find out their value? If they are valuable but you do not want to sell them yet, what would you do with them?

_____

_____

_____

7. In the 1990s, some people thought that tiny stuffed animals, plastic action figures, and Japanese trading cards would be big collectibles in the future. What items on sale today do you think will be popular collectibles in the future? Explain your reasoning.

_____

_____

_____

Calculator: Finding What Percent One Number Is of Another

You can use a calculator to find what percent one number is of another. Remember, on some calculators you may need to enter the ⬚ = key after the ⬚ % key.

Example 1: 60 is what percent of 75?

Procedure	Calculator Entry	Calculator Display
Step 1 Enter 60.	6 0	60.
Step 2 Enter the ÷ key.	÷	60.
Step 3 Enter 75 and the % key.	7 5 %	80.

So, 60 is 80% of 75.

If your calculator does not have a ⬚ % key, multiply by 100 instead.

Example 2: 90 is what percent of 40?

Procedure	Calculator Entry	Calculator Display
Step 1 Divide 90 by 40.	9 0 ÷ 4 0 =	2.25
Step 2 Multiply by 100.	× 1 0 0 =	225.

So, 90 is 225% of 40.

Practice

Use a calculator to find the answers.

1. 45 is what percent of 90? _____

2. 5 is what percent of 20? _____

3. 250 is what percent of 50? _____

Name _____ Date _____

Use a calculator to find the answers.

4. 110 is what percent of 550? _____

5. 27 is what percent of 0.45? _____

6. $68.40 is what percent of $22.80? _____

7. $3.25 is what percent of $125? _____

8. $18.60 is what percent of $2.50? _____

Use a calculator to solve.

9. Julio earns $2,400 per month. He pays $600 in rent. What percent of his monthly pay goes for rent?

_____

10. Sally has budgeted $960 for travel expenses. She has already spent $120. What percent has she spent?

_____

11. Frank saved $2.25 of each $25 he earned. What percent of his income did he save? _____

12. Of 25 students enrolled in a course, 4 transferred out. What percent of the students remained in the course? _____

13. Anthony earns $420 per week. He saves $63 each week to buy a motorcycle. What percent of his earnings does Anthony save? _____

14. Joanna budgeted $50 for her cell phone bill this month. She actually spent $57. What percent of her cell phone budget did Joanna spend? _____

15. The Montalvos have budgeted $650 for food this month. They have already spent $143 on food. What percent of their food budget have the Montalvos spent? _____

16. Vanessa budgeted $250 for dental expenses this year. Her actual expenses were $185. What percent of her dental budget did Vanessa spend?

_____

Part II Review

Vocabulary

Circle the letter of the words(s) that completes the sentence.

1. The percent that prices increase is called the _____.

   a. Inflation rate   **b.** CPI   **c.** Purchasing power

2. The expenses that vary from month to month are called _____.

   a. Living expenses   **b.** Fixed expenses   **c.** Net income

3. An organized plan for spending money is called a(n) _____.

   a. Liability   **b.** Annual expense   **c.** Budget

Skills

Find the answer.

4. Gayle buys a pair of boots priced at $48.50. The sales tax rate is 7%.

   a. How much sales tax does Gayle pay? Round to the nearest cent. _____

   b. What is the total cost of the boots? _____

5. Nate buys an umbrella priced at $14.55. The sales tax rate is $8\frac{1}{2}\%$.

   a. How much sales tax does Nate pay? Round to the nearest cent. _____

   b. What is the total cost of the umbrella? _____

6. A price went from $87 to $93. What was the inflation rate to the nearest tenth of a percent?

   _____

7. A price went from $7.39 to $7.99. What was the inflation rate to the nearest tenth of a percent?

   _____

8. What is the purchasing power of $17,800 after 3% inflation? _____

9. What is the purchasing power of $30,300 after 2.5% inflation? _____

10. The Scotts spent $396, $408, and $472 over the past 3 months on food. To the nearest dollar, how much should they budget next month for food? _____

11. Patrick spent $93, $72, and $86 over the past 3 months on gas. To the nearest dollar, how much should he budget next month for gas? _____

Find the answer.

12. What is the monthly share of an annual $5,832 expense? _____

13. The Swider family made a budget. They allotted their income as follows: food, 0.14; housing 0.28; clothing, 0.06; savings, 0.10; transportation, 0.21; entertainment, 0.04; medical care, 0.08; other, 0.09. For which types of expense did they allot more than 0.15 of their budget? _____

14. The Wallaces' net monthly income is $3,120 and their total monthly expenses are $3,328. By how much do they need to reduce their monthly expenses to have a balanced budget? _____

Use the monthly budget for problems 15–17.

15. Find the monthly share of annual expenses. _____

16. Find the total monthly budget for all expenses. _____

17. What is the balance for this monthly budget? _____

MONTHLY BUDGET	
Living expenses	$978
Fixed expenses	$1,006
Annual expenses	$852
Net income	$2,573

Use the table of estimated costs for raising a family on page 61 for problems 18–19.

18. What will it cost to raise a child that will be born 3 years from now from birth to age 18? _____

19. What will it cost to raise a child that will be born 2 years from now from age 5 to age 18 and pay for 4 years of private college tuition? _____

Don's house and its contents are worth $186,300. He has $8,362 in checking/savings/cash, and his car is worth $8,364. Don has balances of $94,382 on this mortgage, $5,380 on his auto loan, and $3,172 on his credit card. Find Don's:

20. Total assets. _____   **21.** Total liabilities. _____   **22.** Net worth. _____

The Mathematics of Personal Finance and Investment, SV 9780547625683

Part II Test

Find the sales tax. Round to the nearest cent.

1. Purchase price: $20.88
   Sales tax rate: 5% _____

2. Purchase price: $59.95
   Sales tax rate: $4\frac{1}{2}\%$ _____

Find the inflation rate to the nearest tenth of a percent.

3. Original price: $153
   Current price: $167 _____

4. Original price: $2.39
   Current price: $2.89 _____

Find the purchasing power after inflation.

5. Net income: $19,300
   Inflation rate: 1.5% _____

6. Net income: $27,078
   Inflation rate: 4% _____

Find the amount to budget for May.

7. Past electricity expenses:
   Feb., $48; March, $52; April, $71

   _____

8. Past food expenses:
   Feb., $432; March, $416; April, $427

   _____

Use the monthly budget for problems 9–11.

9. Find the monthly share of annual expenses. _____

10. Find the total monthly budget for all expenses. _____

11. By how much would the net monthly income need to increase to have a balanced budget? _____

MONTHLY BUDGET	
Living expenses	$1,351
Fixed expenses	$1,108
Annual expenses	$7,092
Net income	$2,984

Solve.

12. The Brown family made a budget. They allotted $\frac{7}{20}$ of their income for housing. What percent of their income did they allot for housing? _____

13. Some experts estimate that it will cost $211,710 to raise a child born next year to age 18. Find the average yearly cost of raising the child to age 18. Round to the nearest $1,000. _____

The Roberts' house and its contents are worth $173,600. They have $9,136 in checking/savings/cash, and their car is worth $10,980. They have balances of $80,950 on their mortgage, $9,340 on their auto loan, and $11,870 on other loans. Find the Roberts':

14. Total assets. _____

15. Total liabilities. _____

16. Net worth. _____

Part III:
Investments

Pre-Skills Test

Subtract.

1. $1,287.50 − $1,000 = _____

2. $87.23 − $50 = _____

3. $564.32 − $500 = _____

4. $7,384.24 − $5,000 = _____

5. $38.74 − $36.42 = _____

6. $49.21 − $47.04 = _____

7. $85.03 − $79.57 = _____

8. $104.77 − $99.38 = _____

Multiply.

9. $\frac{1}{2} \times$ $1,000 = _____

10. $\frac{1}{2} \times$ $75 = _____

11. $4 \times$ $31.54 = _____

12. $5 \times$ $37.48 = _____

13. $50 \times$ $2.64 = _____

14. $250 \times$ $4.83 = _____

15. $0.0165 \times$ $1,000 = _____

16. $0.0232 \times$ $5,000 = _____

17. $0.0112 \times$ $2,500 = _____

18. $0.0548 \times$ $10,000 = _____

Divide.

19. $10,000 ÷ $50 = _____

20. $975 ÷ $1,000 = _____

21. $1,850 ÷ $2,000 = _____

22. $129.60 ÷ 4 = _____

23. $518.40 ÷ 12 = _____

24. $11,544 ÷ 12 = _____

Name _____ Date _____

Rename as a decimal.

25. $\frac{3}{4}$ _____

26. $\frac{1}{8}$ _____

27. $\frac{1}{2}$ _____

28. $\frac{7}{8}$ _____

29. 4.83% _____

30. 5.14% _____

31. $2\frac{3}{4}\%$ _____

32. $3\frac{3}{8}\%$ _____

Rename as a percent.

33. 0.054 _____

34. 0.0535 _____

35. 0.0394 _____

36. 0.9975 _____

Find the answer to the nearest cent.

37. 8.75% of $2,500 _____

38. 7.739% of $459.50 _____

39. $5\frac{3}{4}\%$ of $4,000 _____

40. $6\frac{1}{2}\%$ of $7,420.80 _____

Find the answer to the nearest tenth of a percent.

41. $43.85 is what percent of $250? _____

42. $983.50 is what percent of $1,000? _____

43. $135.38 is what percent of $500? _____

44. $1,218.49 is what percent of $1,000? _____

The Mathematics of Personal Finance and Investment, SV 9780547625683

U.S. Savings Bonds

A popular form of investing money is through the purchase of **Series EE United States Savings Bonds**. These bonds are issued by the U.S. federal government. Many people give savings bonds as gifts.

Paper Series EE Savings Bonds are available with **face values** of $50; $75; $100; $200; $500; $1,000; $5,000; and $10,000. Paper bonds are purchased for $\frac{1}{2}$ of their face value.

Example 1: What is the cost of a paper Series EE Savings Bond with a face value of $500?

THINK: The purchase price is $\frac{1}{2}$ of the face value.

Multiply.

$\frac{1}{2} \times \$500 = \$250$

A $500 savings bond will cost $250.

An EE Savings Bond is guaranteed to reach its face value by its maturity date. The maturity date is 20 years after the bond is purchased. The bond will then continue to earn interest at a fixed interest rate for an additional 10 years.

Savings bonds can be redeemed, or cashed in, at any time after 1 year from the purchase date. The table shows the values of a $50 paper EE Savings Bond if it were to be redeemed at various times.

REDEMPTION VALUE OF $50 PAPER SAVINGS BOND
(Purchase date: May 2005)

Years Held	Value
0.5	Could not be redeemed
1.0	$25.66
1.5	$26.10
2.0	$26.56
2.5	$27.04
3.0	$27.50
3.5	$27.98
4.0	$28.46
4.5	$28.98
5.0	$29.74
5.5	$30.26
6.0	$30.78

The Mathematics of Personal Finance and Investment, SV 9780547625683

Example 2: How much would you receive if you redeemed a $200 paper savings bond purchased in May 2005 after 6 years?

| Step 1 | Use the table on page 81. After 6 years, a $50 bond can be redeemed for $30.78.

| Step 2 | Divide to find how many units of $50 are in $200.

$200 \div \$50 = 4$

| Step 3 | Multiply the value of a $50 bond by 4.

$4 \times \$30.78 = \$123.12$

The $200 bond could be redeemed for $123.12.

Example 3: How much interest was earned on the $200 paper savings bond redeemed after 6 years?

> Interest Earned = Redemption Value − Purchase Price

Subtract.

$123.12 − \$100 = \$23.12$

The bond earned $23.12 in interest.

Think About It

1. Who pays the interest on U.S. Savings Bonds?

_____

_____

2. Why are U.S. Savings Bonds considered to be "patriotic" investments?

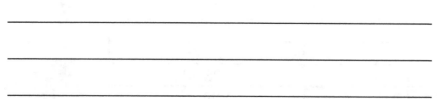

Practice

Remember to estimate whenever you use your calculator.

Find the cost of buying the paper bonds.

Face value of bond	Number of bonds	Purchase price
$100	1	**1.** _____
$75	1	**2.** _____
$50	4	**3.** _____
$500	2	**4.** _____
$1,000	3	**5.** _____
$5,000	5	**6.** _____

Find the redemption value of the paper bond purchased in May 2005.

Face value of bond	Years held	Redemption value
$500	3.0	**7.** _____
$500	4.5	**8.** _____
$5,000	5.0	**9.** _____
$1,000	4.0	**10.** _____
$100	2.5	**11.** _____
$75	4.5	**12.** _____

Complete the table for paper bonds purchased in May 2005.

Bonds held	Years held	Redemption value	Interest earned
3 $500 bonds	$3\frac{1}{2}$	**13.** _____	**14.** _____
2 $100 bonds	4	**15.** _____	**16.** _____
2 $1,000 bonds	$5\frac{1}{2}$	**17.** _____	**18.** _____
5 $50 bonds	$4\frac{1}{2}$	**19.** _____	**20.** _____
8 $5,000 bonds	6	**21.** _____	**22.** _____
6 $75 bonds	1	**23.** _____	**24.** _____
7 $10,000 bonds	$4\frac{1}{2}$	**25.** _____	**26.** _____

Name _____   Date _____

Complete the table for paper bonds purchased in May 2005.

Bonds held	Years held	Redemption value	Interest earned
3 $100 bonds	4	27. _____	28. _____
4 $200 bonds	2	29. _____	30. _____
2 $500 bonds	$4\frac{1}{2}$	31. _____	32. _____
5 $75 bonds	5	33. _____	34. _____
6 $1,000 bonds	$3\frac{1}{2}$	35. _____	36. _____
2 $10,000 bonds	4	37. _____	38. _____
5 $5,000 bonds	$5\frac{1}{2}$	39. _____	40. _____

Solve.

41. Karen bought a paper U.S. Savings Bond with a face value of $500 in May 2005.

  a. How much did Karen pay for the bond?

  _____

  b. If Karen redeemed the bond after 2 years, how much would she receive? _____

  c. If Karen redeemed the bond after 5 years, how much would she receive? _____

  d. How much more interest would Karen earn if she redeemed the bond after 5 years than after 2 years? _____

42. Juan bought a paper U.S. Savings Bond with a face value of $100 in May 2005.

  a. How much did Juan pay for the bond?

  _____

  b. If Juan redeemed the bond after 6 years, how much would he receive? _____

  c. If Juan redeemed the bond after 20 years, how much would he receive? _____

  d. How much more interest would Juan earn if he redeemed the bond after 20 years than after 6 years? _____

The Mathematics of Personal Finance and Investment, SV 9780547625683

Certificates of Deposit

You can purchase another investment called a **certificate of deposit**, or **CD**, at your bank. Because money invested in a CD cannot be withdrawn for a set period of time without a penalty charge, CDs earn higher interest rates than regular savings accounts.

CDs can usually be purchased for $500 or more. Common terms for CDs are 3 months, 6 months, 1 year, 3 years, and 5 years. In general, the longer the term, the higher the interest rate, but the longer you do not have ready access to your money.

The table shows how one bank advertises its CDs. Since interest is usually compounded daily, you can use the **annual effective yield** to find the actual interest earned in a year. The annual effective yield can also be used to compare CDs with the returns on other investments.

CERTIFICATES OF DEPOSIT

Term	Annual rate	Annual effective yield
3 months	0.60%	0.60%
6 months	1.00%	1.00%
1 year	1.24%	1.25%
3 years	1.83%	1.85%
5 years	2.37%	2.40%

Example 1: How much interest will you earn on a 1-year $5,000 CD?

Step 1 Use the table.

The annual effective yield for a 1-year CD is 1.25%.

Step 2 Multiply to find the interest.
THINK: 1.25% = 0.0125

0.0125 × $5,000 = $62.50

You will earn $62.50 in interest on the CD.

Name _____ Date _____

The annual effective yield must be divided by 2 for 6-month terms and by 4 for 3-month terms.

Example 2: How much interest will you earn on a 3-month $2,000 CD?

| Step 1 | Use the table on page 85.

The annual effective yield for a 3-month CD is 0.60%.

| Step 2 | Multiply to find the annual interest.
THINK: 0.60% = 0.0060

$0.0060 \times \$2,000 = \$12$

| Step 3 | Divide to find the 3-month interest.
THINK: 3 months is $\frac{1}{4}$ of a year.

$\$12 \div 4 = \$3$

You will earn $3 in interest on the CD.

Think About It

1. Why do CDs earn more interest than regular savings accounts?

_____

_____

_____

2. Why might some people be hesitant to purchase longer-term CDs?

_____

_____

_____

Practice

Remember to estimate whenever you use your calculator.
Use the table on page 85. What is the annual effective yield for the CD?

1. 3-month CD _____   2. 3-year CD _____

3. 5-year CD _____   4. 6-month CD _____

Use the table on page 85. Find the interest earned over the term.

Amount invested	Term of CD	Interest earned
$2,500	1 year	**5.** _____
$1,000	1 year	**6.** _____
$7,500	6 months	**7.** _____
$5,000	3 months	**8.** _____
$1,500	1 year	**9.** _____
$10,000	6 months	**10.** _____

Use the table on page 85. Solve.

11. Michael invested $15,000 in a 6-month CD. After 6 months, he took his interest and reinvested the $15,000 in another 6-month CD.

  a. How much interest did Michael earn on the first CD? _____

  b. How much interest did he earn on the second CD? _____

  c. How much interest did he earn in all? _____

12. Nancy invested $15,000 in a 1-year CD.

  a. How much interest did Nancy earn? _____

  b. Did the 1-year CD earn more or less than the two 6-month CDs in Exercise 11? How much more or less? _____

13. Sonya invested $5,000 in a 3-month CD. After 3 months, she took her interest and reinvested the $5,000 in another 3-month CD.

  a. How much interest did Sonya earn on the first CD? _____

  b. How much interest did she earn on the second CD? _____

  c. How much interest did she earn in all? _____

14. Manual invested $5,000 in a 6-month CD.

  a. How much interest did Manual earn? _____

  b. Did the 6-month CD earn more or less than the two 3-month CDs in Exercise 13? How much more or less? _____

Name _____ Date _____

The annual yield of any investment is calculated by dividing the interest earned in 1 year by the amount invested.

Example: In 1 year, you earned $124.25 in interest on an investment of $2,000. To the nearest tenth of a percent, what was the annual yield?

Step 1 | Divide.

$124.25 \div $2,000 = 0.062125$

Step 2 | Rename the decimal as a percent.

$0.062125 \approx 6.2\%$

The annual yield was 6.2%.

Find the annual yield of each investment to the nearest tenth of a percent.

Amount invested	Interest earned in 1 year	Annual yield
$500	$11.25	1. _____
$1,500	$20.85	2. _____
$2,000	$64.20	3. _____
$2,500	$71.00	4. _____
$5,000	$151.00	5. _____
$10,000	$238.00	6. _____

Solve. Round each percent to the nearest tenth.

7. In 1 year, you earned $37.80 in interest on a $3,000 CD and $48.50 on a $5,000 savings account.

   a. What was the annual yield for the CD? _____

   b. What was the annual yield for the savings account? _____

   c. Which investment had the greater yield? _____

Corporate Stocks

Another form of investment is buying **corporate stocks** that are traded on a stock exchange. A **share** of stock is a piece of ownership in a corporation. Owners of stocks are paid **dividends** on their shares when the corporation makes a profit.

Investors also make or lose money when they sell their stocks, depending on whether the price has gone up or down. Stocks can be purchased or sold through stockbrokers, and you can keep track of how your stocks are doing by reading the stock tables in the financial sections of many online newspapers.

Example 1: Part of a stock exchange listing is shown below. Identify the column headings.

Highest and lowest prices over past year

Annual dividend per share in dollars

Yield = Dividend ÷ Price

Number of shares sold in 1000s

Highest and lowest prices of the day

Current or most recent price

Change in price from the previous day's closing

52-week					Vol				
High	Low	Stock	Div	Yld	1,000s	High	Low	Last	Chg
53.02	29.77	EagleT	1.12	2.4	109	45.78	45.05	45.78	+0.46
40.53	30.20	EastUtil	2.30	7.2	213	32.21	31.75	31.89	−0.13
25.35	14.82	Echmer	0.56	3.3	1,532	17.03	18.74	17.02	—
31.50	20.78	Ecotab	0.58	2.0	212	29.35	28.89	28.87	−0.61
19.86	14.34	EDA	0.28	1.8	141	15.50	15.23	15.40	+0.14
43.98	33.00	EdisWr	1.80	4.8	60	37.26	36.75	37.26	+0.72
85.14	52.12	EGadw	2.52	2.9	1,286	87.01	84.10	87.01	+2.10
37.88	27.65	EGH	0.56	1.6	883	34.80	34.12	34.74	+0.47
13.70	6.12	Eldar	0.22	1.6	124	13.52	13.26	13.52	—
18.00	12.47	Elgon		—	70	14.33	14.00	14.24	−0.25
3.02	1.38	Elsant		—	166	2.26	2.17	2.25	—
18.00	10.48	EmprA		—	971	16.01	15.65	15.82	−0.32
26.00	13.15	Encrsh	0.80	3.3	922	24.51	24.00	24.26	−0.20
43.24	30.75	Enhart	1.40	3.2	594	43.76	42.64	43.37	+0.72
50.60	37.85	Enrin	2.48	5.5	630	45.02	44.75	45.00	+0.23
22.62	14.37	EntB		—	287	22.05	20.98	22.05	+1.60
10.89	8.72	EqtBl	0.50	5.3	134	9.47	9.38	9.36	−0.22
10.05	6.07	Equitax	0.16	2.0	33	7.97	7.85	7.87	−0.25
12.74	6.20	ERan		—	955	7.15	6.87	7.05	−0.15
16.48	9.50	ERN		—	108	13.99	13.53	13.53	−0.34
42.37	29.05	EssWt	0.72	1.7	41	42.52	42.03	42.52	+0.68
20.27	10.28	Estren		—	41	16.47	16.25	16.25	−0.50
32.23	15.98	EthyPr	0.40	1.3	1,081	29.92	29.32	29.75	—
92.03	57.50	ExetRf	3.60	4.0	6,132	89.60	89.14	89.51	+0.13

Example 2: You decide to buy 50 shares of Empire Airfreight (EmprA). How much will the shares cost?

| Step 1 | Use the stock listing to find that the current price for EmprA is $15.82.

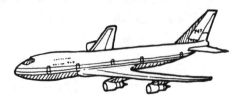

| Step 2 | Multiply to find the cost.

50 × $15.82 = $791

The stock will cost $791.

Example 3: You purchased 40 shares of Ethyl Products (EthyPr) at $16.84 per share. How much profit will you make if you sell the shares at the current price?

| Step 1 | Use the stock listing to find that the current price for EthyPr is $29.75.

| Step 2 | Subtract to find the increase for each share.

$29.75 − $16.84 = $12.91

| Step 3 | Multiply to find the profit.

40 × $12.91 = $516.40

You will make a profit of $516.40.

Example 4: You own 250 shares of Exeter Refining (ExetRf). How much did you receive in dividends over the past year on these shares? To the nearest tenth of a percent, what was your rate of return (yield) on your investment over the past year?

| Step 1 | Use the stock listing to find that ExetRf paid a dividend of $3.60 per share and that the current price is $89.51.

| Step 2 | Multiply to find your earnings.

250 × $3.60 = $900

| Step 3 | Multiply to find the value of your investment.

250 × $89.51 = $22,377.50

| Step 4 | Divide to find your return.

$900 ÷ $22,377.50 ≈ 0.0402 ≈ 4.0%

You received $900 in dividends, representing a 4.0% return on your investment.

Name _____ Date _____

1. What causes stocks to go up or down in price?

_____

_____

_____

2. What is meant by a "bull" market and a "bear" market?
   (Research these terms on the Internet if needed.)

_____

_____

_____

Practice

Remember to estimate whenever you use your calculator.
Use the stock listing on page 89 to answer.

1. What was the highest price Elgon was traded at over the past year? _____

2. What was the lowest price Enhart was traded at over the past year? _____

3. How many shares of ERN were traded on this particular day? _____

4. By how much did a share of Equitax decline from its 52-week high? _____

5. How much did Eastern Gadwick (EGadw) pay per share in dividends? _____

6. What was the day's high price for Enrin? _____

7. What is the current price of Ecotab? _____

8. How has the price of Eastern Utility (EastUtil) changed from the previous day's closing?

_____

9. Which 3 stocks reached their highest prices in a year?

_____

_____

Name _____ Date _____

Use the stock listing on page 89 to find the current cost of the shares.

Stock	Number of shares held	Current cost
Eldar	75	10. _____
EntB	30	11. _____
EastUtil	125	12. _____
EDA	65	13. _____
Estren	250	14. _____
EagleT	2,300	15. _____

Complete the table.

Purchase price	Last price	Number of shares	Amount of profit (P) or loss (L)
$14.50	$21.74	30	16. _____
$25.80	$19.23	80	17. _____
$84.36	$125.52	50	18. _____
$64.00	$42.89	250	19. _____

Use the stock listing on page 89 to complete the table.

Stock owned	Dividend per share	Total annual dividend	Rate of return
10 shares of EGH	20. _____	21. _____	22. _____
40 shares of EdisWr	23. _____	24. _____	25. _____
75 shares of EssWt	26. _____	27. _____	28. _____
500 shares of EDA	29. _____	30. _____	31. _____

Solve.

32. Carey bought 25 shares of a stock when it was priced at $25.39 per share. Later that same year, she sold the stock when it was priced at $31.58 per share. She received a dividend of $0.16 per share while she owned the stock.

a. How much did Carey pay for the stock? _____

b. How much profit did Carey make when she sold the stock? _____

c. How much did Carey receive in dividends from the stock? _____

The Mathematics of Personal Finance and Investment, SV 9780547625683

Problem Solving Application: Trading Stocks

If you buy shares of stock in a corporation, you own part of the corporation. The prices of many different stocks are updated regularly in many online newspapers and on other financial Websites.

The table below shows data about six corporations. Notice that the price (in dollars) of a share is written as a decimal.

52-Week		Stock	High	Low	Last	Change
High	Low					
9.13	6.85	Nasco	8.50	7.73	8.23	+0.22
62.34	55.00	NES	60.02	56.85	57.14	−1.25
115.12	100.49	Nostro	110.62	105.34	106.99	+1.62
92.23	83.50	Noxco	87.53	85.47	86.50	−1.00
94.53	80.21	NR	92.05	86.89	87.06	−2.51
45.50	34.20	NYA	42.22	40.20	42.00	+1.47
The highest and lowest prices during the last 52 weeks		Names of corporations are often abbreviated	Today's highest and lowest prices		Current or most recent price	The change from yesterday's closing price to the most recent price + increase/− decrease

Example: What was the closing price yesterday of a share of NYA stock?

THINK: To find yesterday's closing price, subtract the change from the current or most recent price.

Current or most recent price of 1 share of NYA stock	−	Change from yesterday's closing price	=	Yesterday's closing price of 1 share of NYA stock
42.00	−	1.47	=	40.53

So, the closing price yesterday of a share of NYA stock was $40.53.

Practice

Find the most recent price for each stock according to the report on page 93.

1. Nasco _____

2. Noxco _____

3. NES _____

4. NR _____

Is the most recent price of a share of stock an increase or decrease from yesterday's closing price?

5. NYA _____

6. Nostro _____

7. Noxco _____

8. NES _____

Solve.

9. Which of the 6 stocks has the highest current price? _____

10. Which of the 6 stocks has the lowest current price? _____

11. How many of the 6 stocks decreased in price from yesterday to now? _____

12. Which stock increased in price by $1.62 from yesterday to now? _____

13. What are the 52-week high and low prices for Nasco? _____

14. What is the difference between the 52-week high and low prices for Nasco? _____

15. What is the current price of 10 shares of NYA stock? _____

16. Was yesterday's closing price for Noxco higher than yesterday's closing price for NR? _____

17. If you bought 100 shares of Nostro stock at yesterday's closing price and sold it at the current price, how much would your profit or loss be? _____

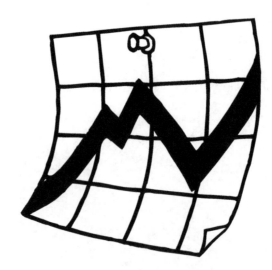

Corporate and Municipal Bonds

Another form of investment is buying **corporate bonds** or **municipal bonds**. When corporations need to raise large sums of money for such things as factory expansions and when states and cities need money for such things as roads or schools, they issue bonds.

When you buy a bond, you are really lending the corporation or the government your money, based on an agreement that you will be paid interest over the life of the bond and that you will be repaid the full amount when the bond matures.

The face value of a bond, often $1,000, is called the **par value**. The **maturity date** of the bond, often 5 years, 10 years, or 20 years, is when the bond can be redeemed at par value.

However, many investors buy and sell bonds on the bond market before the bonds reach maturity. Bonds are sold on the bond market at the bond's **market price**, which may be higher or lower than the par value.

BONDS

Bond	Maturity Date	Interest rate	Market price
Excelsior Corporation	2021	5.50%	$978
Roadway Company	2016	3.45%	$1,019
State of Ohio	2019	4.50%	$1,025

Use the bond table on the previous page.

Example 1: At what percent of par are the Excelsior Corporation bonds currently selling?

THINK: $1,000 par value bonds are selling for $978.

Divide to find the percent.
$978 ÷ $1,000 = 0.978 = 97.8%

The bonds are currently selling for 97.8% of par.

Example 2: How much interest would you receive per year if you owned 8 State of Ohio $1,000 bonds?

THINK: Interest is paid on the par value, not on the market price.

| Step 1 | Multiply to find the interest on 1 bond.

4.50% of $1,000 = 0.0450 × $1,000 = $45

| Step 2 | Multiply to find the interest on 8 bonds.

8 × $45 = $360

You would earn $360 annually in interest.

Example 3: What is the current yield on a $1,000 Roadway Company bond? Round to the nearest tenth of a percent.

Current Yield = Annual Interest ÷ Market Price

| Step 1 | Multiply to find the annual interest.

3.45% of $1,000 = 0.0345 × $1,000 = $34.50

| Step 2 | Divide to find the current yield.

$34.50 ÷ $1,019 ≈ 0.0338 ≈ 3.4%

The current yield is 3.4%

Name _____ Date _____

1. How are bonds different from stocks?

_____

_____

_____

2. How are municipal bonds different from corporate bonds?

_____

_____

Practice

Remember to estimate whenever you use your calculator.

BONDS

Bond	Maturity Date	Interest rate	Market price
Chapman International	2019	8.50%	$1,199
City of Yuma	2025	4.13%	$891
Dover Products	2020	7.75%	$953
Eastern Metals	2021	5.30%	$1,022
Finch Township	2030	5.25%	$1,004

Use the bond listing above. Which bond(s):

1. Has the earliest maturity? _____

2. Is currently the most expensive? _____

3. Has the lowest interest rate? _____

4. Has the highest interest rate? _____

5. Are selling below par? _____

6. Are selling above par? _____

Find the current cost of the bonds.

7. 4 Dover Products bonds _____

8. 8 Finch Township bonds _____

9. 20 Eastern Metals bonds _____

10. 15 City of Yuma bonds _____

At what percent of par is the $1,000 bond currently selling?

11. Market price: $950 _____

12. Market price: $875 _____

13. Market price: $837.50 _____

14. Market price: $1,500 _____

15. Market price: $1,050 _____

16. Market price: $1,125 _____

Find the annual interest you would earn each year from the bonds.

17. 6 Chapman International $1,000 bonds _____

18. 10 City of Yuma $1,000 bonds _____

19. 30 Eastern Metals $1,000 bonds _____

20. 50 Finch Township $1,000 bonds _____

Find the current yield on the bond to the nearest tenth of a percent.

21. Chapman International _____

22. City of Yuma _____

23. Dover Products _____

24. Finch Township _____

Mutual Funds

Rather than selecting your own mixture of stocks and other investments, you can pool your money with other investors and buy shares in a **mutual fund**. When the fund earns money on its investments, the profits are paid to investors in the fund in the form of **dividends**.

Most mutual funds have a **sell price** that represents the value of a share and a **buy price** that is usually higher than the sell price, since it includes a sales charge.

According to the mutual fund listing below, a share of Corvette Fund can be sold for $23.17, it can be purchased for $24.76, and its value decreased by $0.06 per share from the previous day.

MUTUAL FUNDS

Fund	Sell	Buy	Chg
Allegiance	10.31	10.74	+0.09
Americana	15.07	NL	+0.07
Cornell	13.98	15.28	−0.04
Corvette	23.17	24.76	−0.06
Criteria	17.18	NL	+0.14
Dayton	6.95	7.24	−0.03
Forecast	7.38	7.85	+0.07
Future	24.12	NL	−0.11
Generation	10.25	11.01	+0.02
Guard	36.54	38.12	+0.16
Hanover	16.45	NL	−0.03
International	12.83	14.12	+0.08
Keymark	9.56	NL	−0.14
NL means No Load (Buy price is equal to sell price.)			

Name _____ Date _____

Example 1: What will it cost to buy 80 shares of the Hanover Fund?

THINK: Since the fund is no load (NL), the buy price is the same as the sell price.

Multiply to find the price.
$80 \times \$16.45 = \$1,316$

80 shares will cost $1,316.

Example 2: An investor sells 250 shares of the Forecast Fund. What is the current value of those shares?

THINK: The sell price for a share of the fund is $7.38.

Multiply to find the value.
$250 \times \$7.38 = \$1,845$

The 250 shares are currently worth $1,845.

Think About It

1. What are the advantages of investing in a mutual fund rather than buying individual stocks or bonds?

_____

_____

_____

Practice

Remember to estimate whenever you use your calculator.

Use the mutual funds listing on page 99. Complete the table.

Fund	Cost to buy 1 share	Cost to buy 50 shares	Cost to buy 250 shares
Guard	1. _____	2. _____	3. _____
Criteria	4. _____	5. _____	6. _____
Cornell	7. _____	8. _____	9. _____
Future	10. _____	11. _____	12. _____

Name _____ Date _____

Use the mutual funds listing on page 99.
Find the current value of the mutual fund shares.

13. 400 shares of Allegiance _____

14. 1,500 shares of Keymark _____

15. 550 shares of Generation _____

16. 40 shares of Dayton _____

17. 2,200 shares of Americana _____

18. 750 shares of International _____

19. 30 shares of Criteria _____

20. 85 shares of Guard _____

Solve.

21. An investor has $4,000 to invest in a mutual fund. To the nearest whole share, how many shares of the Forecast Fund can be bought? _____

22. An investor has $12,000 to invest in a mutual fund. To the nearest whole share, how many shares of the Hanover Fund can be bought? _____

23. An investor has $1,500 to invest in a mutual fund. To the nearest whole share, how many shares of the International Fund can be bought? _____

24. An investor bought 400 shares of the Generation Fund at $8.17 per share. If the shares are sold at today's price, how much profit will be made?

_____

25. An investor bought 650 shares of the Criteria Fund at $21.74 per share. If the shares are sold at today's price, how much of a loss will there be?

_____

26. An investor bought 200 shares of the Keymark Fund at $9.48 per share. If the shares are sold at today's price, how much profit will be made?

_____

Name _____ Date _____

Use the mutual funds listing.

MUTUAL FUNDS

Fund	Sell	Buy	Chg
Ameron	9.23	9.68	+0.11
Carmel	16.61	NL	+0.08
Dorell	14.18	16.09	−0.04
Gordon	18.96	NL	+0.02
Marcus	28.31	30.34	+0.05
Oceana	13.27	NL	+0.08
Revere	12.67	13.68	+0.07
NL means No Load (Buy price is equal to sell price.)			

Complete the table.

Fund	Cost to buy 1 share	Cost to buy 50 shares	Cost to buy 250 shares
Revere	27. _____	28. _____	29. _____
Dorell	30. _____	31. _____	32. _____
Carmel	33. _____	34. _____	35. _____

Find the current value of the mutual fund shares.

36. 200 shares of Ameron _____

37. 1,200 shares of Gordon _____

38. 50 shares of Oceana _____

39. 300 shares of Carmel _____

Solve.

40. An investor has $5,000 to invest in a mutual fund. To the nearest whole share, how many shares of the Revere can be bought? _____

41. An investor bought 750 shares of the Gordon Fund at $20.45 per share. If the shares are sold at today's price, how much of a loss will there be?

_____

Retirement Plans

Some employees are automatically enrolled in a **pension plan** that provides them with a **pension** after they retire. Most pension plans combine employee payroll deductions with employer contributions that are invested in stocks, bonds, or mutual funds.

Many pension benefits can be calculated using the formula and the benefit percent table below.

$$\text{Annual Pension Benefit} = \text{Benefit Percent} \times \text{Years of Service} \times \text{Average Annual Earnings}$$

BENEFIT PERCENT FOR EACH YEAR OF SERVICE

Years of Service	Age 55	56	57	58	59	60	61	62	63	64	65+
5 to 9	0	0	0								
10	1.00	1.06	1.12	1.20	1.30	1.40	1.52	1.64	1.76	1.88	2.00
11	1.07	1.12	1.18	1.25	1.35	1.44	1.55	1.66	1.78	1.89	2.00
12	1.13	1.18	1.24	1.31	1.39	1.48	1.58	1.69	1.79	1.90	2.00
13	1.20	1.25	1.29	1.36	1.44	1.52	1.62	1.71	1.81	1.90	2.00
14	1.26	1.31	1.35	1.41	1.48	1.56	1.65	1.74	1.82	1.91	2.00
15	1.33	1.37	1.41	1.47	1.53	1.60	1.68	1.76	1.84	1.92	2.00
16	1.40	1.43	1.47	1.52	1.58	1.64	1.71	1.78	1.86	1.93	2.00
17	1.46	1.49	1.53	1.57	1.62	1.68	1.74	1.81	1.87	1.94	2.00
18	1.53	1.56	1.58	1.62	1.67	1.72	1.78	1.83	1.89	1.94	2.00
19	1.59	1.62	1.64	1.68	1.71	1.76	1.81	1.86	1.90	1.95	2.00
20	1.66	1.68	1.70	1.73	1.76	1.80	1.84	1.88	1.92	1.96	2.00
21	1.73	1.74	1.76	1.78	1.81	1.84	1.87	1.90	1.94	1.97	2.00
22	1.79	1.80	1.82	1.84	1.85	1.88	1.90	1.93	1.95	1.98	2.00
23	1.86	1.87	1.87	1.89	1.90	1.92	1.94	1.95	1.97	1.98	2.00
24	1.93	1.93	1.93	1.94	1.94	1.96	1.97	1.98	1.98	1.99	2.00
25 or over	2.00	2.00	2.00	2.00	2.00	2.00	2.00	2.00	2.00	2.00	2.00

Example 1: A worker retires at age 59 with 18 years of service in the company. If her average annual earnings were $35,000, what is her annual pension benefit? How much will she receive per month?

Step 1 Use the table on the previous page. The benefit percent for a 59-year-old with 18 years of service is 1.67.

Step 2 Use the formula to find the annual benefit.

$1.67\% \times 18 \times \$35,000 = \$10,521$

Step 3 Divide to find the monthly benefit.

$\$10,521 \div 12 = \$876.75$

This worker will receive a pension of $10,521 per year, or $876.75 per month.

Workers whose do not have pension plans are often able to save for retirement using a 401(k) plan. A **401(k)** is a type of retirement savings account offered by many corporations. The employee makes contributions to the account, and the employer may match all or part of the employee's contributions.

Employees decide how to invest their contributions by choosing among the investment options offered by the plan. Many plans include a variety of mutual funds as well as the opportunity to purchase company stock.

Example 2: Eddie decides to contribute 6% of his salary to a 401(k) plan. His annual salary is $42,000, and he is paid twice per month. How much will Eddie contribute to his 401(k) plan each pay period?

Step 1 Find the annual amount Eddie contributes.

$6\% \text{ of } \$42,000 = 0.06 \times \$42,000 = \$2,520$

Step 2 Divide to find the amount per pay period.
THINK: Eddie is paid twice per month, so he has 24 pay periods in one year.

$\$2,520 \div 24 = \$105$

Eddie will contribute $105 to his 401(k) each pay period.

Example 3: The table describes the 401(k) matching program offered by Elaine's company. Elaine contributes 5% of her annual salary of $36,000 to her 401(k) plan. How much will her company contribute to her 401(k) each year?

401(k) Match Program

For every $1.00 the employee contributes,...	...the employer contributes $0.50.*
*The maximum employer contribution is 4% of the employee's salary.	

Step 1 Find the annual amount Elaine contributes.

5% of $36,000 = 0.05 × $36,000 = $1,800

Step 2 Divide to find the annual amount the company contributes.
THINK: The company contributes half of what Elaine does, so divide by 2.

$1,800 ÷ 2 = $900

The company will contribute $900 to Elaine's 401(k) each year.

Individual Retirement Accounts (or **IRAs**) allow people to save for retirement on their own. Contributions to an IRA can be used to purchase a wide variety of investments, including stocks, bonds, mutual funds, and certificates of deposit.

In a **traditional IRA**, contributions are often tax-deductible, meaning that you pay no income tax on the money you put into the IRA. However, withdrawals from the account at retirement are taxed as income.

By contrast, in a **Roth IRA**, contributions are not tax-deductible, but withdrawals from the account at retirement are usually tax-free.

The table shows the maximum yearly contribution allowed to an individual's IRAs in 2011.

Age at end of 2011	Maximum IRA contribution (for most individuals)
Under 50	$5,000
50 or older	$6,000

Example 4: In 2011, Sherri was 46 years old. She contributed $3,500 to her traditional IRA. What is the maximum amount she could contribute to her Roth IRA?

Step 1 Use the table to find Sherri's maximum yearly contribution.

THINK: Since Sherri is under 50, her maximum contribution amount is $5,000.

Step 2 Subtract Sherri's contribution to her traditional IRA.

$5,000 − $3,500 = $1,500

Sherri could contribute a maximum of $1,500 to her Roth IRA.

Think About It

1. Why does an employee's contributions to his or her pension fund represent only a small part of the eventual pension benefits?

_____

_____

2. What is one advantage that a 401(k) plan may have over an IRA?

_____

_____

3. Why might someone choose to invest in a traditional IRA over a Roth IRA?

_____

_____

Practice

Remember to estimate whenever you use your calculator.

Use the benefit percent table on page 103. Complete the table. Round money amounts to the nearest cent.

Age at retirement	Years of service	Average annual earnings	Benefit percent	Annual pension	Monthly pension
65	20	$24,000	1. _____	2. _____	3. _____
57	15	$37,800	4. _____	5. _____	6. _____
58	23	$31,000	7. _____	8. _____	9. _____
63	12	$39,850	10. _____	11. _____	12. _____
69	34	$24,375	13. _____	14. _____	15. _____

Complete the table. Round to the nearest cent.

Annual salary	Percent contributed to 401(k)	Annual contribution to 401(k)	Pay periods per year	Contribution per pay period
$25,000	6%	16. _____	24	17. _____
$38,100	7%	18. _____	12	19. _____
$42,400	10%	20. _____	52	21. _____
$32,900	8%	22. _____	12	23. _____
$29,500	4%	24. _____	26	25. _____

For every $1.00 that an employee contributes to a 401(k) plan, the employer contributes $0.50 (up to a maximum employer contribution of 4% of the employee's salary). Use this information to complete the table.

Annual salary	Percent employee contributes to 401(k)	Amount employee contributes to 401(k)	Amount employer contributes to 401(k)
$27,000	3%	26. _____	27. _____
$33,500	5%	28. _____	29. _____
$36,200	6%	30. _____	31. _____
$44,100	8%	32. _____	33. _____

Name _____ Date _____

Use the table about maximum IRA contributions on page 106. Complete the table.

Age at end of 2011	Traditional IRA contribution in 2011	Maximum Roth IRA contribution in 2011
52	$2,800	34. _____
31	$0	35. _____
46	$4,700	36. _____
63	$5,000	37. _____

Solve.

38. Raymond retires from his company at age 62 after 20 years of service. His average annual earnings were $53,475. Use the benefit percent table on page 103.

a. What is Raymond's benefit percent? _____

b. What is his annual pension benefit? _____

c. How much will he receive per month?

_____

39. Shanna contributes 12% of her salary to a 401(k) plan. Her annual salary is $38,500, and she is paid once per month.

a. What is the annual amount Shanna contributes to her 401(k)? _____

b. How much does she contribute to her 401(k) each pay period? _____

40. For every $1.00 that an employee contributes to a 401(k) plan, the employer contributes $0.25 (up to a maximum employer contribution of 3% of the employee's salary).

a. Mark contributes 6% of his annual salary of $28,000 to the 401(k) plan. What is the annual amount that he contributes? _____

b. What is the annual amount that the company contributes to Mark's 401(k) plan? _____

c. What is the total annual contribution to Mark's 401(k)? _____

The Mathematics of Personal Finance and Investment, SV 9780547625683

Problem Solving Strategy: Working Backward

Situation:

Edie wants to make one investment now so that she will have $24,000 to take a luxury cruise around the world when she retires in 18 years. She invests in a mutual fund in which her money is expected to double every 9 years. How much money should Edie initially invest in order to have $24,000 in 18 years?

Strategy:

Working backward can help you find a solution.

Applying the Strategy:

Step 1 What amount should be in Edie's fund at the end of the 9th year so it would double to be $24,000 by the end of the 18th year?

THINK: $\frac{1}{2}$ of $24,000 = $\frac{1}{2} \times$ $24,000 = $12,000

Step 2 What amount should Edie invest initially so that at the end of the 9th year it would double to be $12,000?

THINK: $\frac{1}{2}$ of $12,000 = $\frac{1}{2} \times$ $12,000 = $6,000

Edie should initially invest $6,000.

Name _____ Date _____

Roy invests money once in a real-estate partnership. It is expected that his money will triple every 7 years. He wants to have $108,000 in 21 years to set up his own business.

1. Explain how you can work backward to determine how much money Roy should initially invest.

_____

_____

_____

_____

2. How much should Roy initially invest? _____

Practice

Remember to estimate whenever you use your calculator.
Solve by working backward.

Alice wants to have $40,000 saved to help pay for her daughter's college education 18 years from now. She invests in a corporate bond fund in which her money is expected to double every 9 years.

1. What amount should be in Alice's fund at the end of the 9th year so it would double to be $40,000 by the end of the 18th year? _____

2. What amount should Alice initially invest so that at the end of the 9th year it would double to be $20,000? _____

Ted wants to make one investment now so that he will have $45,000 for the down payment on a house in 16 years. He invests in a mutual fund in which his money is expected to double every 8 years.

3. What amount should be in Ted's fund at the end of the 8th year so it would double to be $45,000 by the end of the 16th year? _____

4. What amount should Ted initially invest so that at the end of the 8th year it would double to be $22,500? _____

Name _____   Date _____

Ben invests money once in a stock income fund. It is expected that the money in his account will triple every 8 years. Ben wants to have $81,000 in 24 years to supplement his retirement income.

5. What amount should be in Ben's account at the end of the 16th year so it would triple to be $81,000 by the end of the 24th year? _____

6. What amount should be in Ben's account at the end of the 8th year so it would triple to be $27,000 by the end of the 16th year? _____

7. What amount should Ben initially invest so that at the end of the 8th year it would triple to be $9,000?

_____

Richard invests money once in a municipal bond fund. It is expected that the money in his account will triple every 11 years. Richard wants to have $54,000 in 33 years to purchase land for a small farm.

8. What amount should be in Richard's account at the end of the 22nd year so it would triple to be $54,000 by the end of the 33rd year? _____

9. What amount should be in Richard's account at the end of the 11th year so it would triple to be $18,000 by the end of the 22nd year? _____

10. What amount should Richard initially invest so that at the end of the 11th year it would triple to be $6,000? _____

11. Susan wants to have $100,000 saved to begin investing in real estate 20 years from now. She invests in a fund she expects to double her money every 10 years. How much money should Susan invest in the fund? _____

12. Beth wants to have $36,000 saved to start her own business 12 years from now. She invests money once in a bond fund. She expects her money to double every 6 years. How much money should Beth initially invest? _____

The Mathematics of Personal Finance and Investment, SV 9780547625683

13. Roberto buys a zero coupon bond for his newborn grandson. It is expected that the money will double every 12 years. How much should Roberto spend on the bond so that his grandson will have $75,000 in 36 years? _____

14. Carla wants to have $108,000 saved to help pay for her son's college education 14 years from now. She invests a corporate bond fund in which her money is expected to double every 7 years. How much money should Carla initially invest in the fund?

_____

15. Alicia wants to have $35,000 saved to help pay for some property in 15 years. Her mutual funds are expected to double her money every $7\frac{1}{2}$ years. How much should Alicia initially invest in the funds?

_____

16. Helga invests money in a fund in which her money is expected to double every 7.5 years. How much money should Helga invest now if she wants to have $200,000 for retirement in 30 years? _____

17. Martin wants to have $270,000 saved for his retirement $37\frac{1}{2}$ years from now. He invests in a stock and bond portfolio in which his money is expected to triple every $12\frac{1}{2}$ years. What should Martin initially invest in the portfolio?

_____

18. Helene buys a corporate bond for her new granddaughter. It is expected that the money will double every $7\frac{1}{2}$ years. How much should Helene spend on the bond so that her granddaughter will have $70,000 in 15 years? _____

Decision Making: Buying Stocks

Louis and Rebecca O'Rourke decide to invest some of their money in the stock market.

PROBLEM

Louis and Rebecca decide to start with a $3,000 investment. They visit a stockbroker and ask for the names of a variety of technology companies. They take the list and use the stock listings from a financial Website to prepare the following table. In which stock or stocks should they invest?

New Era	$37.50/share	20¢ dividend	Up $5/share in past year	High risk
Geoparts	$87.37/share	$2.75 dividend	Down $20/share in past year	Moderate risk
Techno	$3.87/share	No dividend	Up 50¢/share in past year	Moderate risk
Laserpert	$15.25/share	$1.75 dividend	Up $4.50/share in past year	Low risk
Jetstorm	$117.75/share	$4.50 dividend	Down $2/share in past year	Low risk
Phantom	$21.50/share	$1.00 dividend	Up $3.00/share in past year	High risk

DECISION-MAKING FACTORS

• Yield (Dividends ÷ Price)

• Growth prospects

• Risk

Name _____ Date _____

DECISION-MAKING COMPARISONS

Compare the 6 stocks by completing the table. Round percents to the nearest tenth of a percent.

Stock	Price per share	Dividend per share	Yield	Percent increase (I) or decrease (D) in price over past year	Risk
New Era	1. _____	$0.20	2. _____	3. _____	4. _____
Geoparts	5. _____	6. _____	7. _____	8. _____	Moderate
Techno	$3.87	9. _____	10. _____	11. _____	12. _____
Laserpert	13. _____	14. _____	11.5%	15. _____	16. _____
Jetstorm	17. _____	18. _____	19. _____	1.7% (D)	20. _____
Phantom	21. _____	22. _____	23. _____	24. _____	25. _____

MAKING THE DECISIONS

Which stock should Lois and Rebecca buy if the only factor were:

26. Lowest price? _____

27. Highest dividend? _____

28. Highest yield? _____

29. Greatest recent percent growth? _____

30. Which stock should be purchased if Louis and Rebecca wish to minimize risk and maximize yield? _____

31. Which stock should be purchased if Louis and Rebecca are willing to take high risks and wish to maximize yield? _____

32. Which stock(s) are probably the safest investments? Why?

_____

_____

33. Louis and Rebecca decide to place half of their investment in a low-risk, low-yield investment and half of their investment in a high-risk, high-yield investment. How many shares of which stocks should they buy?

_____

34. How would you invest the $3,000? Why?

_____

_____

The Mathematics of Personal Finance and Investment, SV 9780547625683

Name _____ Date _____

PROBLEM

Carole and Ben decide to invest $3,500 in stocks. They narrow their choices to 6 utility companies and list some information about each stock. Now, they must decide which stocks they should invest in.

State Gas	$22.50/share	$1.00 dividend	Up $2.00/share in past year	High risk
Ray G & E	$75.67/share	$2.25 dividend	Down $18.50/share in past year	Moderate risk
NeoElec	$4.89/share	No dividend	Up 50¢/share in past year	Low risk
Franklin	$124.25/share	$4.50 dividend	Down $3/share in past year	High risk
Tor G & E	$16.50/share	$2.00 dividend	Up $4.75/share in past year	Low risk
New Gas	$39.45/share	60¢ dividend	Up $4/share in past year	Moderate risk

DECISION-MAKING COMPARISONS

Compare the 6 stocks by completing the table. Round percents to the nearest tenth of a percent.

Stock	Price per share	Dividend per share	Yield	Percent increase (I) or decrease (D) in price over past year	Risk
State Gas	35. _____	$1.00	36. _____	37. _____	38. _____
Ray G & E	39. _____	40. _____	41. _____	42. _____	Moderate
NeoElec	$4.89	43. _____	44. _____	45. _____	46. _____
Franklin	47. _____	48. _____	3.6%	49. _____	50. _____
Tor G & E	51. _____	52. _____	53. _____	40.4% (I)	54. _____
New Gas	55. _____	56. _____	57. _____	58. _____	59. _____

The Mathematics of Personal Finance and Investment, SV 9780547625683

Name _____ Date _____

MAKING THE DECISIONS

Which stock should Carole and Ben buy if the only factor were:

60. Lowest price? _____

61. Highest dividend? _____

62. Highest yield? _____

63. Greatest recent percent growth? _____

64. Which stock should be purchased if Carole and Ben wish to minimize risk and maximize yield? _____

65. Which stock should be purchased if Carole and Ben are willing to take high risks and wish to maximize yield? _____

66. Which stock(s) are probably the safest investments? Why?

_____

_____

67. Carole wants to place half of their investment in a low-risk, high-yield investment and half of their investment in a moderate-risk, high-yield investment. How many shares of which stocks should Carole and Ben buy if they choose Carole's plan?

_____

_____

68. Ben wants to place half of their investment in a low-risk, high-recent-percent-growth investment and half of their investment in a moderate-risk, high-recent-percent-growth investment. How many shares of which stocks should Carole and Ben buy if they choose Ben's plan?

_____

_____

69. How would you invest the $3,500? Why?

_____

_____

Money Tips 2

Self-employed persons can invest in and manage their own retirement plans.

LET'S LOOK AT THE FACTS

Many companies have retirement plans for their employees. Self-employed persons can establish similar plans for themselves. One type is called a **Keogh profit-sharing plan**, which allows you to invest varying amounts of your net earned income (NEI).

If you want to keep your contributions to a Keogh profit-sharing plan tax-deductible, there is a limit to how much you can contribute each year. In 2011, the limit was 25% of your net earned income or $49,000 per year, whichever was less. The formulas shown below can be used to calculate your NEI and your contribution amounts.

$$\text{Net Earned Income} = \frac{\text{Net Profits}}{1 + \% \text{ of Contribution}}$$

$$\text{Plan Contribution} = \text{Net Earned Income} \times \% \text{ of Contribution}$$

LET'S DISCUSS WHY

1. Why do you think it would be a good idea for self-employed persons to invest in a retirement plan?

_____

_____

2. You are not required to contribute to a retirement plan every year. What might be some reasons for not contributing in some years?

_____

_____

3. If 25% of your NEI in one year were $18,000, what would your total annual NEI be?

_____

The Mathematics of Personal Finance and Investment, SV 9780547625683

4. If your annual NEI is \$40,000, what would your plan contribution be if you invest:

    a. 5% of it? _____

    b. 8% of it? _____

    c. 12% of it? _____

5. Tax-deductible contributions to a Keogh profit-sharing plan are considered business expense deductions. How would this affect the taxes paid by a self-employed person?

_____

_____

LET'S SEE WHAT YOU WOULD DO

6. You are a freelance artist. Last year, you earned \$35,000, and you invested 5% of it in a Keogh profit-sharing plan. This year you will earn about the same amount of money, but would like to invest 10% of it. Your expenses this year, however, are higher.

    What are your options, and which do you think would be the most financially wise option to choose?

_____

_____

_____

_____

7. You have been investing in a tax-deferred Keogh profit-sharing plan since age 38. You are now age 64, healthy, and able to continue working. Discuss the advantages and disadvantages of retiring.

_____

_____

_____

Estimation Skill: Overestimates and Underestimates of Products and Quotients

The symbols $+$ and $-$ may be used to show that an actual product is greater than or less than an estimate.

Example 1:

$$38 \quad \times \quad 295$$
$$\downarrow \qquad \qquad \downarrow$$
$$40 \quad \times \quad 300 = 12,000$$

THINK: Each factor was rounded up, so the actual product is less than 12,000.

Final estimate: $12,000^-$

Example 2:

$$9.2 \quad \times \quad 5.327$$
$$\downarrow \qquad \qquad \downarrow$$
$$9 \quad \times \quad 5 = 45$$

THINK: Each factor was rounded down, so the actual product is greater than 45.

Final estimate: 45^+

Example 3:

$$18 \quad \times \quad \$74.45$$
$$\downarrow \qquad \qquad \downarrow$$
$$20 \quad \times \quad \$70 = \$1,400$$

THINK: One factor was rounded up, and one was rounded down. It is not immediately clear whether $1,400 is high or low. Keep the first estimate.

Final estimate: $1,400

Name _____ Date _____

Estimated quotients can be adjusted in a similar way.

Example 4:

$$822 \quad \div \quad 21$$
$$\downarrow \qquad\qquad \downarrow$$
$$800 \quad \div \quad 20 = 40$$

First estimate: 40

THINK: $21 \times 40 = 840$

Since $840 > 822$, the actual quotient is less than 40.

Final estimate: 40^-

Example 5:

$$\$142.98 \quad \div \quad 28$$
$$\downarrow \qquad\qquad \downarrow$$
$$\$150 \quad \div \quad 30 = \$5$$

First estimate: $5

THINK: $28 \times \$5 = \$140$

Since $\$140 < \$142.98$, the actual quotient is greater than $5.

Final estimate: $\$5^+$

Practice

Estimate the product or quotient. Where appropriate, use the symbol + or − to indicate whether the actual answer is greater than or less than the estimate.

1. 49×66 _____

2. 32×325 _____

3. 58×315 _____

4. $27 \times \$2.98$ _____

5. $18 \times \$2.29$ _____

6. $31 \times \$21.50$ _____

7. 4.2×9.3 _____

8. 6.7×19.38 _____

9. 5.25×7.854 _____

10. $616 \div 32$ _____

11. $855 \div 42$ _____

12. $4,316 \div 81$ _____

13. $\$38.60 \div 20$ _____

14. $\$74.16 \div 25$ _____

15. $\$560.98 \div 72$ _____

16. $9.15 \div 2.8$ _____

Name _____   Date _____

Problem Solving Strategy: Solving a Simpler Problem

Situation:

Bernard invests in stocks. Last year, his income from investments was $4,176.85. This year, his income from investments was $643.25 less than it was last year. What was the total income from his investments for the 2 years?

Strategy:

Sometimes it helps to solve a simpler problem. Using rounded numbers can make the situation seem easier. Often, you can also break a problem into steps and write an equation for each step.

Applying the Strategy:

You do not know this year's income from investments. So, first you need to find that income. Then you can find the total income for the 2 years.

Step 1 Let x represent the investment income this year.
THINK: $643.25 is about $600.

$4,176.85 is about $4,000.

Income Last Year − $600 = Income This Year
$$\$4,000 - \$600 = x$$
$$\$3,400 = x$$

Bernard's income this year was about $3,400.

Step 2 Let t represent the total income from investments.

Income Last Year + Income This Year = Total Income
$$\$4,000 \quad + \quad \$3,400 \quad = \quad t$$
$$\$7,400 \quad = \quad t$$

Bernard's total investment income for the 2 years was about $7,400.

Name _____ Date _____

Now solve the problem using the actual numbers.

Step 1 | Let x represent the investment income this year.

Income Last Year − $643.25 = Income This Year
$4,176.85 − \$643.25 = x$
$3,533.60 = x$

Bernard's income this year was $3,533.60.

Step 2 | Let t represent the total income from investments.

Income Last Year   +   Income This Year   = Total Income
$4,176.85   +   \$3,533.60   =   t$
$7,710.45   =   t$

Bernard's total investment income for the 2 years was $7,710.45.

Practice

Remember to estimate whenever you use your calculator.
Circle the letter of the better choice for simplifying the problem.

1. Don invests in stocks. Last year, his income from investments was $2,630.50. This year, his income from investments was $792.25 more than it was last year. What was the total income from the investments in the 2 years?

a. $\$2,600 − \$800 = x$
       $\$1,800 = x$

$\$2,600 + \$1,800 = t$
       $\$4,400 = t$

b. $\$2,600 + \$800 = x$
       $\$3,400 = x$

$\$2,600 + \$3,400 = t$
       $\$6,000 = t$

2. Stella earns $21,216 per year. This is 2.6 times as much as her younger sister, Tina, earns. What is the difference between their incomes?

a. $\$21,000 = 3t$
       $\$7,000 = t$

$\$21,000 − \$7,000 = d$
       $\$14,000 = d$

b. $t = 3 \times \$21,000$
       $t = \$63,000$

$\$63,000 − \$21,000 = d$
       $\$42,000 = d$

Solve by writing a simpler problem.

3. Al and Ben are brothers. They are saving to buy a video game system. Al saves $13.75 per week. Ben saves $2.75 less per week than Al does. In all how much money do the two brothers save each week?

Estimate: _____

Exact answer: _____

4. Winona invests in stocks. Last year, her income from investments was $2,750. This year, her income from investments was 2.1 times as great as last year. What was the total income from her investments in the 2 years?

Estimate: _____

Exact answer: _____

5. Karen earns $50,232 per year at her job as a firefighter. This is 4.6 times as much as her son earns. What is the difference between their incomes?

Estimate: _____

Exact answer: _____

6. For 3 years, Marianne has been depositing money in a special bank account. During the third year, she deposited $3,960. This amount was $935 more than she deposited during the second year. The third-year amount was 2.4 times as much as she deposited during the first year. What was the total amount that she deposited during the 3 years?

Estimate: _____

Exact answer: _____

Name _____   Date _____

Solve by writing a simpler problem.

7. Joshua invests in mutual funds. Last year, his income from mutual funds was $824. This year, his income from mutual funds was $618 more than last year. What was the total income from his mutual funds in the 2 years?

   Estimate: _____

   Exact answer: _____

8. Ruth and Louis Pike are saving for a vacation. Ruth saves $25.50 per week. Louis saves $5.25 less per week than Ruth does. In all how much money does the couple save each week?

   Estimate: _____

   Exact answer: _____

9. Last year, Manuela contributed $3,820 to her 401(k) account. This year, she contributed 1.8 times as much as last year. What was the total amount that Manuela contributed to her 401(k) in the 2 years?

   Estimate: _____

   Exact answer: _____

10. Martina earns $679 per month at her job as a fast food worker. Her father earns 5.5 times what Martina earns. What is the difference between their monthly earnings?

    Estimate: _____

    Exact answer: _____

11. The cost of a share of Aldatec is $24.20. The cost of a share of Telagen is 3.6 times the cost of a share of Aldatec. What is the difference between the cost of a share of Telagen and the cost of a share of Aldatec?

    Estimate: _____

    Exact answer: _____

Part III Review

Vocabulary

Circle the letter of the words(s) that complete the sentence.

1. Investments that allow you to pool your money with other investors and buy a variety of stocks or other investments are called _____.

   a. Certificates of deposit   **b.** Mutual funds   **c.** Corporate bonds

2. Investments that are really loans to the federal government are called _____.

   a. Savings bonds   **b.** 401(k) plans   **c.** Certificates of deposit

3. One type of retirement plan offered by many employers is called a(n) _____.

   a. Corporate stock   **b.** IRA   **c.** 401(k) plan

Skills

Find the answer.

4. Warren redeemed a $500 paper U.S. Savings Bond for $389.67. How much interest did he earn on the bond? _____

5. How much interest will Jennifer earn on a 6-month $2,000 CD that has an annual effective yield of 1.784%? _____

6. What is the cost of 60 shares of a stock selling at $35.60 per share? _____

7. What is the value of 500 shares of a stock trading at $56.13 per share? _____

8. How much profit did Myra make when she bought 30 shares of a stock at $17.75 per share and sold them at $31.32 per share? _____

9. What was the loss when Kevin was forced to sell 150 shares of stock at $27.48 per share that he purchased at $41.74 per share? _____

10. To the nearest tenth of a percent, what is the rate of return on 20 shares of a stock that sells for $46.52 and pays $2.75 in dividends? _____

Find the answer.

11. To the nearest tenth of a percent, what is the yield on a bond that costs $953 and pays $68.93 in interest annually? _____

12. How much interest is earned per year on a $1,000 bond with an interest rate of 6.492%? _____

13. A mutual fund has a buy price of $12.81 per share and a sell price of $13.18 per share. Chita owns 240 shares of the mutual fund. What is the current value of Chita's shares? _____

14. A pension plan pays 2% per year for each year of service. How much will the annual pension benefit be for a woman with 24 years of service and average annual earnings of $47,500? _____

15. A pension plan pays 1.5% per year for each year of service. How much will the annual pension benefit be for a man with 17 years of service and average annual earnings of $36,000? _____

16. Jessie decides to contribute 5% of her salary to a 401(k) plan. Her annual salary is $38,400, and she is paid once per month. How much will Jessie contribute to her 401(k) plan each pay period? _____

17. In 2011, the maximum IRA contribution for individuals aged 50 or older was $6,000. In that year, Dominic was 61 years old. He contributed $2,400 to his Roth IRA. What is the maximum amount he could contribute to his traditional IRA in 2011? _____

18. Sylvia wants to make one investment now so that she will have $32,000 for the down payment on a house in 16 years. She invests in a mutual fund in which her money is expected to double every 8 years. How much money should Sylvia initially invest? _____

19. Edgar invests in corporate bonds. Last year, his income from bonds was $948.29. This year, his income from bonds was $123.72 less than it was last year. What was the total income from his bonds for the 2 years?

_____

Part III Test

Complete the table.

Purchase price of stock	Last price of stock	Number of shares	Amount of profit (P) or loss (L)
$25.62	$33.51	40	**1.** _____
$14.77	$11.25	75	**2.** _____
$92.39	$108.45	60	**3.** _____
$55.50	$49.73	150	**4.** _____

Solve.

5. If a $50 paper U.S. Savings Bond can be redeemed for $38.89 after 6 years, how much will a $1,000 paper U.S. Savings Bond be worth after 6 years?

_____

6. How much interest is earned on a $3,000 6-month CD that offers an effective annual yield of 1.36%?

_____

7. What is the cost of 125 shares of a stock selling at $59.32 per share? _____

Use the table to solve.

52-Week		Stock	High	Low	Last	Change
High	**Low**					
8.73	5.92	BEX	7.85	7.63	7.79	+0.18
54.31	43.22	SRC	52.40	52.21	52.40	−0.84
102.75	93.38	MLL	99.85	96.13	99.85	+1.02

8. What is the difference between the 52-week high and low prices for SRC? _____

9. What is the current price of 15 shares of BEX stock? _____

10. If you bought 50 shares of MLL stock at yesterday's closing price and sold it at the current price, how much would your profit or loss be? _____

Name _____ Date _____

Solve.

11. How much interest is earned per year on a $1,000 bond that pays an interest rate of 5.831%? _____

12. How much would it cost to buy 25 shares of a no-load mutual fund with a selling price of $16.14 per share? _____

13. A pension plan pays 2% per year for each year of service. How much will the monthly pension benefit be for a worker with 28 years of service and average annual earnings of $28,000? Round to the nearest cent._____

14. Colby's company has a 401(k) matching program. For every $1.00 the employee contributes, the employer contributes $0.50. Colby contributes 8% of his annual salary of $30,000 to his 401(k) plan. How much will his employer contribute to his plan each year? _____

15. You want to have $48,000 saved in 18 years. The fund you invest in expects to double your money after 9 years. How much should you initially invest in the fund? _____

16. Last year, Pedro contributed $2,400 to his Roth IRA. This year, he contributed 2.2 times as much as last year. What was the total amount that Pedro contributed to his Roth IRA in the 2 years?

_____

Use the following information to answer problems 17–20.

You decide to invest $1,000 in one of the following:
  a. A stock selling for $14.50 per share that pays $1.00 per share in dividends.
  b. A corporate bond that pays an interest rate of 8.52%.
  c. A mutual fund selling for $28.75 per share that pays $0.25 per share in dividends.
  d. A 1-year CD with an effective annual yield of 1.62%.

17. To the nearest cent, what are the annual dividends paid on $1,000 of the stock? _____

18. To the nearest cent, what are the annual dividends paid on $1,000 of the mutual fund? _____

19. Which offers the higher yield, the stock or the mutual fund? _____

20. How much more interest will the corporate bond pay per year than the CD? _____

Support Materials

Group Projects 130

    What's in a Receipt............................ 131

    Making a Budget................................ 132

    Mutual Funds 133

Practice Forms 134

    Budget Sheet 135

    Asset and Liability Worksheets 136

    Investment Analysis Tables.................. 137

Charts... 138

    Simple Interest 139

    Compound Interest 140

    Investment Risk and Return.................. 142

    Portfolio Planning for Retirement 143

Glossary... 144

Answer Key 150

Support Materials:
Group Projects

Name _____ Date _____

What's in a Receipt

Using advertisements from grocery stores, each group should make a receipt for a week's worth of groceries. Be sure to include the name, quantity, and price of each item; the subtotal before sales tax; the amount of sales tax; and the total cost of the groceries.

For this activity, assume that your state does not charge sales tax on food sold in grocery stores, but that it does charge 8% sales tax on non-food items, such as shampoo and toothbrushes.

Exchange receipts with another group.

Analyzing the Receipt

Discuss the following with your group.

1. What can you tell about the shopper from the receipt?

 • Do you think the person was shopping for a family or for one person?

 • Do you think the person was planning a party or has pets?

 • What else can you tell about the person? Give reasons to support your analysis.

2. Put the grocery items into categories such as produce, dairy, bakery, frozen foods, and so on. What percent of money was spent on each category?

3. Determine on which items sales tax was charged. For each item that was taxed, how much sales tax was charged?

On Your Own

Think about inflation and how it is likely to affect the shopper's grocery bills in the future.

 • Using the grocery receipt you analyzed, predict what each item on the receipt will cost in 5 years.

 • Predict what the sales tax rate may be in 5 years and apply it to the taxable items.

 • Compare the total in the two receipts. Did the total increase or decrease? What factors do you think contributed to the difference in the totals?

The Mathematics of Personal Finance and Investment, SV 9780547625683

Name _____ Date _____

Making a Budget

For this project, your group will need a number cube and a copy of the budget sheet on page 135.

Sandy and Michael Thompson are a working couple. They want to create a monthly budget so that they know how much they can spend on various expenses. Roll the number cube. Then multiply the number you roll by $500 to determine Sandy's monthly net income. Repeat these steps to determine Michael's net monthly income.

Work with your group to complete a budget sheet for the Thompsons.

Questions to Think About

1. Can the Thompsons afford a mortgage payment (and the other expenses that come with owning a house)? Or would they be better off renting an apartment or a house?

2. Can the Thompsons afford a car payment (and the other expenses that come with owning a car)?

3. Which categories of expenses are absolutely essential, and which categories could the Thompsons do without if needed?

What other questions do you have to think about? Make a list of these questions.

Answering the Questions

Consider the questions in your list. Discuss what information you need to answer them.

• Look at real-estate listings in a local newspaper to determine house and apartment prices in your area. Use an online mortgage calculator to estimate monthly mortgage payments if needed.

• You can use an online auto-loan calculator to estimate the amount of car payments.

• Research average monthly utility costs in your area by visiting the utilities' Websites. Visit the USDA's Website to research average monthly food costs.

Formulating and Implementing the Plan

Organize the information you have gathered.

• Use the information to complete the budget sheet for the Thompsons. Make sure that their total expenses are less than or equal to their total net income.

• Present your budget to the class. Be prepared to support your decisions.

• Discuss how your budget compared to the budgets of other groups. Why do you think there were differences in the budgets developed by different groups?

Name _____ Date _____

Mutual Funds

Mutual funds are often classified according to the kind of investments they invest in. For example, there are stock funds, bond funds, money-market funds, balanced funds, and many others. The goals of each fund are different. Investors should invest in funds that have goals similar to their own.

On Your Own

Look for a listing of mutual funds at a financial Website or an online newspaper. With your group, choose a family of mutual funds to study. (A family of funds is a group of funds offered by the same company.) On your own, do some research about the different types of funds in the family.

- Find out what the funds invest in.

- Based on the risks involved, decide which are conservative funds (low risk) and which are aggressive funds (high risk).

- Show the funds in their appropriate place on a "fund line" like this.

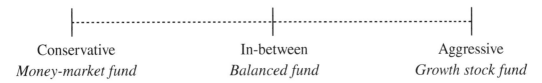

| Conservative | In-between | Aggressive |
| *Money-market fund* | *Balanced fund* | *Growth stock fund* |

Analyzing the Situation

Discuss each situation below with your group. Assume the people in each situation have $5,000 to invest in the family of funds you have been studying. Use your "fund line." Decide which fund or funds would be most appropriate in each situation.

- A young couple wants to invest the money so they will have enough for a down payment on a house in 3 years.

- A couple plans to retire in 5 years. They want to put their money toward retirement.

- The parents of a 13-year-old want to put the money toward the child's college education.

Share your work with the class. Compare the family of funds each group has studied.

- Discuss the variety of funds that are offered within each family of funds.

- Discuss why you would advise the fund or funds you have selected in each of the three situations.

Support Materials:
Practice Forms

Budget Sheet

BUDGET SHEET FOR THE MONTH OF _____
FOR _____

LIVING EXPENSES		FIXED EXPENSES	
Food	_____	Rent	_____
HOUSEHOLD		Mortgage	_____
Electricity	_____	Car Payment	_____
Natural Gas	_____	Savings	_____
Telephone	_____	Contingency	_____
Cell Phone	_____	**TOTAL**	_____
Cable/Internet	_____		
Water	_____	**ANNUAL EXPENSES**	
Other _____	_____	**INSURANCE**	
		Life	_____
TRANSPORTATION		Home	_____
Gas/Oil	_____	Car	_____
Parking/Tolls	_____	Medical/Dental	_____
Repairs	_____	Vacation	_____
Bus/Train/Cab	_____	Property Taxes	_____
Other _____	_____	Home Repairs	_____
		TOTAL	_____
PERSONAL		**MONTHLY SHARE**	_____
Clothing	_____		
Expenses	_____	**MONTHLY SUMMARY**	
Credit Card	_____	**NET INCOME**	_____
		TOTALS	
ENTERTAINMENT		Living	_____
Movies/Sports	_____	Fixed	_____
Eating Out	_____	Annual	_____
TOTAL	_____	**TOTAL EXPENSES**	_____
(LIVING EXPENSES)		**BALANCE**	_____

Support Materials
The Mathematics of Personal Finance and Investment, SV 9780547625683

Asset and Liability Worksheets

Asset Worksheet

ASSETS	
Checking and savings account(s)	_____
Cash	_____
Stocks and bonds	_____
Retirement account(s)	_____
Car	_____
House	_____
Contents of house	_____
Collections, etc. _____	_____
TOTAL ASSETS	_____

LIABILITIES	
Balance on mortgage	_____
Balance on auto loan	_____
Balance on other loans	_____
Balance on credit cards	_____
TOTAL LIABILITIES	_____

The Mathematics of Personal Finance and Investment, SV 9780547625683

Investment Analysis Tables

CD Analysis Table

Amount invested	Term	Annual effective yield	Interest earned

Bond Analysis Table

Bond name	Maturity date	Interest rate	Market price	Annual interest	Current yield

Stock/Mutual Fund Analysis Table

Stock or mutual fund name	Price per share	Dividend per share	Yield	Percent increase (I) or decrease (D) in price over past year	Risk

The Mathematics of Personal Finance and Investment, SV 9780547625683

Support Materials:
Charts

Simple Interest

Simple interest is generally what people think of when, for instance, they consider paying back a small, personal loan "with interest." It is calculated using a simple formula ($p \times r \times t$), and its gains are moderate. Here is a sample table showing the simple interest on a sum of $1,000 at different rates, over various periods.

Showing the interest on $1,000 at various rates.

Days	2.5%	3.0%	3.5%	4.0%	4.5%	5.0%	5.5%	6.0%	6.5%	7.0%	7.5%	8.0%
1	0.0685	0.0822	0.0959	0.1096	0.1233	0.1370	0.1507	0.1644	0.1781	0.1918	0.2055	0.2192
2	0.1370	0.1644	0.1918	0.2192	0.2466	0.2740	0.3014	0.3288	0.3562	0.3836	0.4110	0.4384
3	0.2055	0.2466	0.2877	0.3288	0.3699	0.4110	0.4521	0.4932	0.5342	0.5753	0.6164	0.6575
4	0.2740	0.3288	0.3836	0.4384	0.4932	0.5479	0.6027	0.6575	0.7123	0.7671	0.8219	0.8767
5	0.3425	0.4110	0.4795	0.5479	0.6164	0.6849	0.7534	0.8219	0.8904	0.9589	1.0274	1.0959
6	0.4110	0.4932	0.5753	0.6575	0.7397	0.8219	0.9041	0.9863	1.0685	1.1507	1.2329	1.3151
7	0.4795	0.5753	0.6712	0.7671	0.8630	0.9589	1.0548	1.1507	1.2466	1.3425	1.4384	1.5342
30	2.0548	2.4658	2.8767	3.2877	3.6986	4.1096	4.5205	4.9315	5.3425	5.7534	6.1644	6.5753
31	2.1233	2.5479	2.9726	3.3973	3.8219	4.2466	4.6712	5.0959	5.5205	5.9452	6.3699	6.7945
90	6.1644	7.3973	8.6301	9.8630	11.0959	12.3288	13.5616	14.7945	16.0274	17.2603	18.4932	19.7260
180	12.3288	14.7945	17.2603	19.7260	22.1918	24.6575	27.1233	29.5890	32.0548	34.5205	36.9863	39.4521
360	24.6575	29.5890	34.5205	39.4521	44.3836	49.3151	54.2466	59.1781	64.1096	69.0411	73.9726	78.9041
365	25.0000	30.0000	35.0000	40.0000	45.0000	50.0000	55.0000	60.0000	65.0000	70.0000	75.0000	80.0000

Compound Interest

Compound interest calculations are not as easy to grasp as are simple interest calculations, because they are actually *series* of calculations—that is, with every period, interest is added, and the *result* becomes the input for computing the interest and the new balance. Here is a table showing what happens to a deposited sum of $100 over a period of years, when its interest is compounded once a year:

Year #	Beginning-of-year value	Rate	Earned interest	End-of-year value (after Compounding)
1	$100	10%	$10	$110
2	$110	10%	$11	$121
3	$121	10%	$12.10	$133.10
4	$133.10	10%	$13.31	$146.41
5	$146.41	10%	$14.64	$161.05
6	$161.05	10%	$16.11	$177.16
7	$177.16	10%	$17.72	$194.88
8	$194.88	10%	$19.49	$214.37
9	$214.37	10%	$21.44	$235.81
10	$235.81	10%	$23.58	$259.39

As time goes on, or, if the number of periods is increased, maintaining tables become more time-consuming and less accurate. The chart on p. 141 below shows the amount of interest gained at various interest rates, with various rates of compounding.

As the situation becomes more complicated, a computer will help you keep track of compound interest.

The Mathematics of Personal Finance and Investment, SV 9780547625683

Compound Interest

Compound Interest Table

No. of Periods	0.5%	1%	1.5%	2%	2.5%	3%	3.5%	4%	4.5%	5%
1	1.0050	1.0100	1.0150	1.0200	1.0250	1.0300	1.0350	1.0400	1.0450	1.0500
2	1.0100	1.0201	1.0302	1.0404	1.0506	1.0609	1.0712	1.0816	1.0920	1.1025
3	1.0151	1.0303	1.0457	1.0612	1.0769	1.0927	1.1087	1.1248	1.1412	1.1576
4	1.0202	1.0406	1.0614	1.0824	1.1038	1.1255	1.1475	1.1699	1.1925	1.2155
5	1.0253	1.0510	1.0773	1.1041	1.1314	1.1593	1.1877	1.2167	1.2462	1.2763
6	1.0304	1.0615	1.0934	1.1262	1.1597	1.1941	1.2293	1.2653	1.3023	1.3401
7	1.0355	1.0721	1.1098	1.1487	1.1887	1.2299	1.2723	1.3159	1.3609	1.4071
8	1.0407	1.0829	1.1265	1.1717	1.2184	1.2668	1.3168	1.3686	1.4221	1.4775
9	1.0459	1.0937	1.1434	1.1951	1.2489	1.3048	1.3629	1.4233	1.4861	1.5513
10	1.0511	1.1046	1.1605	1.2190	1.2801	1.3439	1.4106	1.4802	1.5530	1.6289
11	1.0564	1.1157	1.1779	1.2434	1.3121	1.3842	1.4600	1.5395	1.6229	1.7103
12	1.0617	1.1268	1.1956	1.2682	1.3449	1.4258	1.5111	1.6010	1.6959	1.7959
13	1.0670	1.1381	1.2136	1.2936	1.3785	1.4685	1.5640	1.6651	1.7722	1.8856
14	1.0723	1.1495	1.2318	1.3195	1.4130	1.5126	1.6187	1.7317	1.8519	1.9799
15	1.0777	1.1610	1.2502	1.3459	1.4483	1.5580	1.6753	1.8009	1.9353	2.0789
16	1.0831	1.1726	1.2690	1.3728	1.4845	1.6047	1.7340	1.8730	2.0224	2.1829
17	1.0885	1.1843	1.2880	1.4002	1.5216	1.6528	1.7947	1.9479	2.1134	2.2920
18	1.0939	1.1961	1.3073	1.4282	1.5597	1.7024	1.8575	2.0258	2.2085	2.4066
19	1.0994	1.2081	1.3270	1.4568	1.5987	1.7535	1.9225	2.1068	2.3079	2.5270
20	1.1049	1.2202	1.3469	1.4859	1.6386	1.8061	1.9898	2.1911	2.4117	2.6533
21	1.1104	1.2324	1.3671	1.5157	1.6796	1.8603	2.0594	2.2788	2.5202	2.7860
22	1.1160	1.2447	1.3876	1.5460	1.7216	1.9161	2.1315	2.3699	2.6337	2.9253
23	1.1216	1.2572	1.4084	1.5769	1.7646	1.9736	2.2061	2.4647	2.7522	3.0715
24	1.1272	1.2697	1.4295	1.6084	1.8087	2.0328	2.2833	2.5633	2.8760	3.2251
25	1.1328	1.2824	1.4509	1.6407	1.8539	2.0938	2.3673	2.6658	3.0054	3.3864

The Mathematics of Personal Finance and Investment, SV 9780547625683

Investment Risk and Return

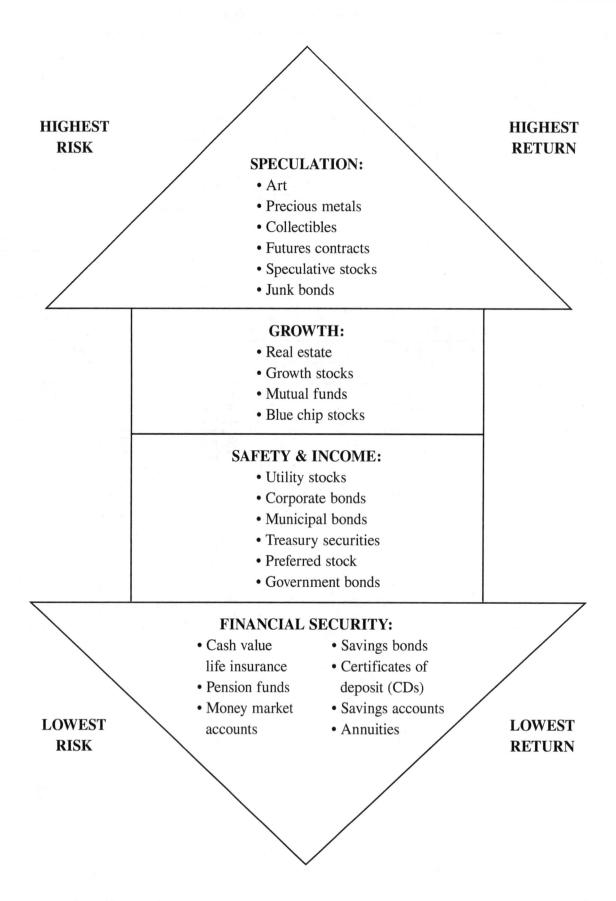

HIGHEST RISK

HIGHEST RETURN

SPECULATION:
- Art
- Precious metals
- Collectibles
- Futures contracts
- Speculative stocks
- Junk bonds

GROWTH:
- Real estate
- Growth stocks
- Mutual funds
- Blue chip stocks

SAFETY & INCOME:
- Utility stocks
- Corporate bonds
- Municipal bonds
- Treasury securities
- Preferred stock
- Government bonds

FINANCIAL SECURITY:
- Cash value life insurance
- Pension funds
- Money market accounts
- Savings bonds
- Certificates of deposit (CDs)
- Savings accounts
- Annuities

LOWEST RISK

LOWEST RETURN

The Mathematics of Personal Finance and Investment, SV 9780547625683

Portfolio Planning for Retirement

There is no guaranteed method for creating a successful retirement portfolio. Successful strategies rely on having the right mix of stocks, bonds and cash. This mixture is known as your "asset allocation."

Stocks provide the most opportunity for long-term growth, but they are volatile, so they can lose you a lot of money in the short term.

Bonds give you weaker long-term returns than stocks, but are safer in the short term.

Cash (CDs, money-market funds, savings accounts) is the least risky of all, but also has the lowest returns.

Most advisors do not recommend cash until after retirement begins. Finding the right mix of stocks and bonds depends on your individual needs, but many advisors start with a basic formula.

$$120 - \text{Your age} = \% \text{ of investments in stocks}$$

The following table shows a slightly more detailed breakdown of suggested investments based on how far off retirement is.

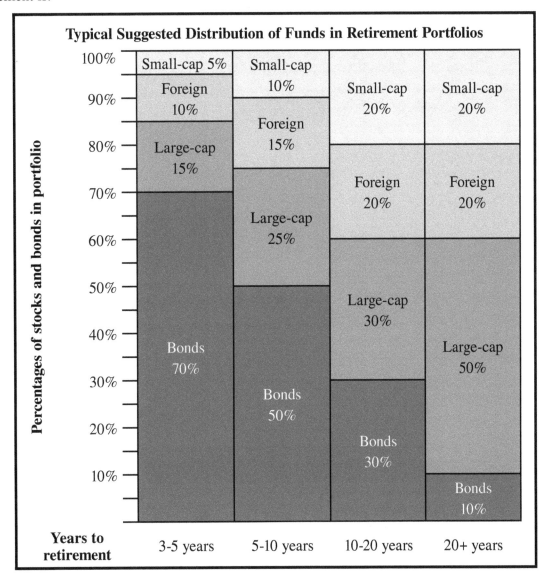

Support Materials:
Glossary

Glossary

addends   Numbers to be added.

annual effective yield   The annual interest rate earned by an investment such as a certificate of deposit, restated as if compounded annually.

annual expense   See budget

asset   See net worth

balanced budget   A budget in which income is equal to expenses.

bar graph   A graph that uses horizontal or vertical bars to display data.

bond   See corporate bond and municipal bond

budget   An organized plan for spending money. **Fixed money expenses**, such as rent, are the same each month and are not easily changed or controlled. **Living expenses**, such as clothing, food, and entertainment, can be changed to some extent according to necessity or choice. **Annual expenses**, such as vacation and insurance premiums, may actually be paid only once a year, but should be shown in the budget in monthly shares.

budget sheet   A form for creating a budget.

buy price   See mutual fund

certificate of deposit (CD)   An investment offered by banks for which depositors agree to keep their money in the account for a specified amount of time in exchange for a fixed interest rate. Depositors face a penalty if money is withdrawn from the account early.

collectible item   Something such as a piece of fine art, stamps, or coins, bought as an investment with the expectation that its value will increase.

Consumer Price Index (CPI)   A number that represents the value of a "market basket" of goods and services bought by a typical city family. Social Security benefits and wages of many union workers change according to how much a dollar will buy (**purchasing power** of a dollar), as indicated by the CPI.

corporate bond   An investment in which a person lends money to a corporation. The holder of the bond is paid interest for a set period of time and is repaid the full amount (**par value**) on the maturity date.

corporate stock   An investment that represents shares in the ownership of a company that is organized as a corporation so that its stock can be traded by stockbrokers on a stock exchange. Owners of stock are paid **dividends** when the corporation makes a profit.

decimal   A base-ten numeral that uses a decimal point and place value.

deflation   The opposite of inflation. During a period of deflation, money is relatively scarce and of greater value. Prices fall, business activity is slowed, and unemployment is high.

difference   The number found by subtracting.

dividend   An amount of money paid to the shareholders of a corporation out of its earnings or to the shareholders of a mutual fund out of the fund's earnings.

dividend in division   See divisor

divisor   The number by which another number, the **dividend**, is divided.
Example: In $6\overline{)24}$, or $24 \div 6$, 6 is the divisor and 24 is the dividend.

estimate   To calculate roughly, when an approximation is sufficient. Used also to check the accuracy of computation.

face value   See United States savings bond

factors   Numbers to be multiplied.

fixed money expense   See budget

401(k)   A type of retirement savings account offered by many corporations. The employee makes contributions to the account, and the employer may match all or part of the employee's contributions.

fraction   The division of two numbers written in the form $\frac{a}{b}$. The denominator (divisor) cannot be 0.
Examples: $\frac{1}{3}$; $\frac{7}{8}$; $\frac{12}{5}$

Individual Retirement Account (IRA)   A type of retirement account that allows people to save for retirement on their own. In a **traditional IRA**, contributions are often tax-deductible, but withdrawals from the account at retirement are taxed as income. In a **Roth IRA**, contributions are not tax-deductible, but withdrawals from the account at retirement are usually tax-free.

inflation   A continuous and relatively large rise in prices caused by expansion in paper money, or bank credit, which decreases the value of money. The **inflation rate** is the percent prices increase, by comparison with a previous month or year.

inflation rate See inflation

Keogh profit-sharing plan A type of retirement plan in which self-employed persons can invest.

liability See net worth

living expense See budget

market price The price at which buyers and sellers trade an item, such as a stock or bond, in a marketplace.

maturity date The date at which the face, or par, value and any remaining interest on a bond is due to the bondholder.

mean (average) A single number used to represent a set of numbers; found by dividing the sum of the numbers by the number of numbers.
Example: Set of numbers: 2, 3, 4, 5, 6
$2 + 3 + 4 + 5 + 6 = 20$ and $20 \div 5 = 4$
4 is the mean.

median The middle value when a set of numbers are listed in order.
Example: 6 is the median of 2, 4, 6, 8, 9.
6 is also the median of 2, 3, 4, 8, 9, 10, since $\frac{4 + 8}{2} = 6$.

mental computation Ways devised to think about operations on numbers so that external help (paper and pencil, calculator) is not needed to arrive at exact answers.

mixed number A number that indicates the sum of a whole number and a fraction.
Example: $3\frac{3}{4} = 3 + \frac{3}{4}$

mode The number that occurs most often in a set of numbers.
Example: 7 is the mode of 1, 1, 4, 7, 7, 7, 8, 9.

municipal bond An investment in which a person lends money to a local (state or city) government. The holder of the bond is paid interest for a set period of time and is repaid the full amount **(par value)** on the maturity date.

mutual fund Money from a group of investors, used to buy and sell a mixture of stocks or other investments. **Dividends** are paid to members of the fund when there are profits. The price of a **share** in the fund goes up or down depending upon the changing value of the investments held. A "no load" funds does not charge a buyer's fee; that is, the **buy price** and **sell price** of a share are the same.

net worth   The difference between what is owned (**assets**) and what is owed (**liabilities**).

order of operations   The order in which an expression is simplified when there is more than one operation.

overestimate   The result when estimating makes the approximation higher than the exact answer can be.

par value   See corporate bond and municipal bond

pension   Money received from a worker's pension plan after the worker retires. The amount received (annual pension benefit) depends upon the number of years the worker has belonged to the pension plan and upon his/her average annual earnings.

pension plan   A retirement plan set up by an employer in which contributions are made a fund set aside for an employee's future retirement.

percent   A ratio that compares a number to 100. 10% means 10 hundredths, or 10 per 100. Example: $75\% = 0.75 = \frac{75}{100}$, or $\frac{3}{4}$

product   The number found by multiplying.

purchasing power   See Consumer Price Index

quotient   The number obtained by dividing.

Example: In $6\overline{)27}$, 4 is the quotient. The **remainder** is 3.

remainder   See quotient

Roth IRA   See Individual Retirement Account

rounded number   A number that is an approximation to a nearest given unit, such as to the nearest hundred, whole number, or tenth.
Examples: 1,721 rounded to the nearest hundred is 1,700.
1.645 rounded to the nearest hundredth is 1.65.
$4\frac{3}{4}$ rounded to the nearest whole number is 5.

sales tax   A percent of the total price of goods and services. The money collected from sales taxes is a major source of income for many state and local governments. Sales tax rates vary from state to state and from city to city.

savings bond See United States savings bond

sell price See mutual fund

Series EE United States savings bond See United States savings bond

share Any of the equal parts into which the stock of a corporation is divided.

stock exchange An organized market for buying and selling stocks and bonds listed by that exchange.

sum The number found by adding.

table An arrangement of information in rows and column
Example:

WEEK OF MARCH 7	
Employee	**Hours worked**
Angela	42
Reed	36

traditional IRA See Individual Retirement Account

underestimate The result when estimating makes the approximation less than the exact answer can be.

United States savings bond (Series EE) Bond issued by the U.S. federal government. Paper bonds are bought at a purchase price that is half the value printed on the face of the bond (the **face value**). Such bonds can be cashed in (redeemed) at any time after 1 year. Paper bonds are guaranteed to reach their face value on or before their maturity date of 20 years.

whole number A number in the set 0, 1, 2, 3, and so one in the same pattern. There is no greatest whole number.

Support Materials:
Answer Key

Answer Key

Pages 8-9
Pre-Skills Test
1. 5; 15   **2.** 8; 12
3. 3; 13   **4.** 7; 17
5. 2; 12   **6.** 9; 19
7. 8; 18   **8.** 6; 16
9. 9   **10.** 8
11. 12   **12.** 10
13. 13   **14.** 8
15. 15   **16.** 6
17. 7   **18.** 7
19. 9   **20.** 4
21. 9   **22.** 7
23. 4   **24.** 28
25. 9   **26.** 40
27. 63   **28.** 16
29. 81   **30.** 20
31. 4   **32.** 3
33. 5   **34.** 7
35. 6   **36.** 9
37. 6   **38.** 5
39. 12   **40.** 16
41. 14   **42.** 27
43. 10   **44.** 4
45. $\frac{4}{15}$ **46.** $\frac{7}{15}$
47. $\frac{4}{15}$ **48.** $\frac{11}{15}$
49. 8%   **50.** 29%
51. 90%   **52.** 4%
53. 34%   **54.** 65%

Pages 12-13
Practice
1. 58.76   **2.** 791
3. 93.98   **4.** 1,552
5. 25.29   **6.** 12.94
7. 7,216   **8.** 39
9. 28.28   **10.** 12
11. 0.2   **12.** 0.47
13. 15,033   **14.** 5,595

15. 89.98   **16.** 495
17. 28.78   **18.** 67.69
19. 3,324   **20.** 4.9
21. 0.14   **22.** 9 R2
23. 4,660   **24.** 6.53
25. 0.3   **26.** 1.7
27. 0.65   **28.** 2.28
29. 3,073 miles
30. $100.71
31. 313 miles
32. $2.88
33. 3,828 miles
34. $92.75
35. $0.12
36. 314 miles

Pages 16-17
Practice
1. 56%   **2.** 4%
3. 119%   **4.** 96%
5. 8.1%   **6.** 200%
7. 0.125; 12.5%
8. 0.75; 75%
9. 0.8; 80%
10. 5.3; 530%
11. 6.5; 650%
12. 2.625; 262.5%
13. 0.57   **14.** 0.41
15. 0.05   **16.** 0.091
17. 0.0008   **18.** 1.61
19. $\frac{1}{10}$ **20.** $\frac{4}{5}$
21. $\frac{11}{20}$ **22.** $1\frac{2}{5}$
23. $1\frac{13}{100}$ **24.** $3\frac{2}{25}$
25. 28   **26.** 27
27. 40   **28.** 31.5
29. 22   **30.** 42
31. 30   **32.** 28.8
33. 60   **34.** 12
35. 1.4   **36.** 14

37. 84 miles
38. 57 questions
39. 45 minutes
40. $206.70
41. $98
42. a. 54 people
   b. 66 people

Page 19
Practice
1. 25
2. 5
3. 20
4. 50
5. See student chart.

Page 21
Practice
1. 22   **2.** 5.1
3. 647   **4.** 68
5. 44   **6.** 0.65
7. 46   **8.** 41
9. 5.7   **10.** 7.9
11. 2   **12.** 4.1
13. 48.3; 31; none
14. 8.6; 9.6; none
15. 551.5; 550; 550
16. 26.2; 26; 38
17. 8.7; 8.2; 8.2
18. 88°F; 89°F; 89°F

Extension
1. 28
2. 69, 70
3. 69
4. a. 621
   b. 272
   c. 134
5. 9.36

Support Materials
The Mathematics of Personal Finance and Investment, SV 9780547625683

Page 23
Think About It
1. Answers may vary.
2. Answers may vary.

Practice
1. 3,848,395
2. 14,711
3. 706
4. 299.132
5. 31,561.504
6. 159.2498
7. 1,414
8. 0.07
9. 14.7
10. 132.2
11. 0.12
12. 0.06
13. 241.369
14. 1.68
15. 3,847 seats
16. $214.50

Page 25
Think About It
1. Answers may vary.

Practice
1. 121
2. 73
3. 593
4. 91¢
5. $8.67
6. 15.82
7. 24
8. 237
9. 39¢
10. $368
11. $4.59
12. 6.12
13. 910
14. 635.7
15. 760
16. 4.27
17. 0.518
18. 0.782
19. $731
20. 0.015 kilograms

Extension
1. 900
2. 12,000
3. 32,000

Page 27
Think About It
1. Answers may vary.
2. Answers may vary.

Practice
1. 1,200
2. 1,820
3. $15
4. $10
5. 190
6. 0.78
7. 83,000
8. 0.054
9. 730
10. 40,000
11. $0.30
12. $16
13. 510
14. 6.7
15. $290
16. $11
17. $100

Page 29
Think About It
1. Answers may vary.

Practice
1. 560,000
2. $4,500
3. $21,000
4. 160
5. 35
6. 250
7. $120
8. 200
9. 0.7
10. 10
11. 2
12. $5
13. $4
14. $10
15. 2
16. 5
17. 10
18. 20
19. $24
20. 4
21. $12,000
22. 10

Page 31
Think About It
1. Answers may vary.
2. Answers may vary.

Practice
1. mental computation
2. paper and pencil or calculator
3. mental computation
4. calculator
5–6. Methods may vary.

5. $8\frac{1}{4}$ feet; mental computation
6. $1,073.50; calculator

Pages 32-33
Part I Review
1. c
2. b
3. a
4. 3,233
5. 87.49
6. 6,430
7. 27,067
8. 69.21
9. 41.49
10. 380
11. 1,506
12. 52.48
13. 1,807
14. 88
15. 0.12
16. 9%
17. 700%
18. 508%
19. 71%
20. 2%
21. 6.8%
22. 0.76
23. 0.059
24. 9
25. 44
26. 27
27. 450
28. 9,753
29. 5,103.9406
30. 6.859
31. 170.69
32. 1,282
33. 12
34. 5.99
35. 37.106
36. 15,000
37. 43
38. 0.28
39. 5,000
40. 5
41. 100
42. 1,438 video game systems
43. $3,864
44. 21 pounds
45. 10 goldfish

Pages 34-35
Part I Test
1. 6,078
2. 77.2
3. 56.4
4. 2,383
5. 41.74
6. 36.47
7. 318
8. 41
9. 7.15
10. 966
11. 5.1
12. 2.64
13. 2.06
14. 0.31

15. 1.14
16. 34%
17. 5.9%
18. 37.5%
19. 125%
20. 132.5%
21. 70%
22. 0.043; $\frac{43}{1,000}$
23. 0.9; $\frac{9}{10}$
24. 1.8; $1\frac{4}{5}$
25. 44.4
26. 45
27. 48
28. 14,078
29. 56.4
30. 2,383
31. 36.47
32. 230.2
33. 106.8
34. 896
35. $1,438
36. 4.2
37. 15
38. $2.01
39. 5,600
40. 3.27
41. 578
42. 6.281
43. 400
44. 300
45. $11
46. 2
47. 3,000
48. 30
49. b
50. c
51. $20.90
52. $7.17
53. 50,000

Part II: Personal Finance
Pages 37-38
Pre-Skills Test
1. $1,294
2. $678.70
3. $913.04
4. $476
5. $177.10
6. $209.03
7. $372,789
8. $365,618
9. $141,131
10. $212,084
11. 78%
12. 6%
13. 19.24%
14. 53.79321%
15. 8.24877%
16. 91.06025%
17. $131.40
18. $120
19. $305.20
20. $795.60
21. $595.68
22. $455.70
23. $2,000
24. $4,000
25. $9,000
26. $50,000
27. $8,000
28. $19,000
29. $45
30. $136

31. $90
32. $143
33. $118
34. $125
35. $200
36. $433
37. $850
38. $650
39. $783
40. $1,333

Pages 40-42
Think About It
Possible answer: People might travel to another state or city to shop because it has a lower sales tax rate. For example, the same $20,000 car will cost less in a state with a 5% sales tax than in one with an 8% sales tax. The hidden costs include the costs of traveling to the other state or city to buy, return, or repair the item.

Practice
1. $0.17
2. $1.37
3. $0.81
4. $1.33
5. $0.15
6. $1.43
7. $1.18
8. $5.94
9. $26.25
10. $7.47
11. $2.58
12. $294.94
13. $1.26
14. $1.28
15. $2.24
16. $2.23
17. $6.48
18. $6.48
19. $0.88
20. $18.38
21. $3.87
22. $89.86
23. $15.42
24. $272.42
25. $394.89
26. $5,181.39
27. $762.21
28. $10,924.96
29. a. $12.80
    b. $172.75
30. a. $2.54
    b. $37.53
31. a. $1.44
    b. $25.44
32. a. $63.98
    b. $977.98

33. a. $67.65
    b. $53.30
    c. $14.35

Pages 44-46
Think About It
1. My income is keeping up with inflation if my percent of pay increase is greater than or equal to the inflation rate.

2. People with fixed incomes can often not keep up with inflation. Because of inflation, their purchasing power decreases over time.

Practice
1. $4.00
2. $16.00
3. $25.00
4. 15.4%
5. 9.6%
6. 4%
7. $15.00
8. $0.41
9. $1.94
10. 16.9%
11. 15.0%
12. 6.1%
13. $675
14. $21,825
15. $984
16. $23,616
17. $575
18. $28,175
19. $454.88
20. $29,870.12
21. $1,220.63
22. $33,654.37
23. $211
24. $41,989
25. a. $0.40
    b. 13.8%
26. a. $0.06
    b. 3.2%
27. a. $3.00
    b. 15.0%
28. $25,740

Extension
1. 16.7%
2. 36.3%
3. 23.3%

4. 8.9%

Pages 48-50
Think About It

1. Possible answer: I can use seasonal changes to predict changes in some living expenses. For example, when it gets cold, the gas bill will be more expensive. When it gets warmer the air conditioner is used, electricity costs will go up.

2. Possible answer: Problems could arise if the annual expense comes due before you have accumulated enough money to pay for it. To avoid this, the monthly share set aside for the annual expense would need to be increased.

Practice

1. $428	**2.** $133
3. $85	**4.** $56
5. $22	**6.** $84
7. $98	**8.** $15
9. $19	**10.** $64
11. $153	**12.** $39
13. $100	**14.** $38
15. $88	**16.** $26
17. $57	**18.** $105
19. $38	**20.** $472
21. $349	**22.** $92
23. $86	**24.** $7
25. $90	**26.** $70
27. $458	**28.** $52
29. $97	**30.** $74

Pages 52-54
Think About It

1. You could reduce expenses, increase income, or both.

2. Possible answer: The amounts in the budget for a single person are usually less than the amounts in the budget for a family. The budget for a single person will almost certainly include lower food and insurance costs than the budget for a family.

Practice

1. $94	**2.** $225
3. $780	**4.** $1,091
5. $945	**6.** $3,492
7. $291	**8.** $2,327
9. $183	**10.** $8

11. a. $6,636
 b. $553
 c. $79

12. a. $1,113
 b. $1,007
 c. $502
 d. $2,622
 e. $112

13. a. $180
 b. $162
 c. $1,458

14. $61	**15.** $325
16. $1,213	**17.** $874
18. $6,480	**19.** $540
20. $2,627	**21.** $463

22. a. $1,309
 b. $577
 c. $3,099
 d. $9

Pages 55-58
Problem Solving Application

1. $\frac{2}{5}$ **2.** $\frac{1}{5}$
3. $\frac{1}{20}$ **4.** $\frac{3}{50}$
5. transportation

6. medical care
7. food
8. savings
9. housing
10. housing
11. entertainment
12. transportation

13. 0.05	**14.** 0.34
15. 0.10	**16.** 0.04
17. 0.03	**18.** 0.24

19. 0.07
20. entertainment
21. mortgage
22. savings
23. health insurance
24. clothing
25. homeowners insurance
26. food
27. health insurance
28. clothing
29. mortgage
30. entertainment

31. 10%	**32.** 22%
33. 4%	**34.** 2%
35. 18%	**36.** 6%

37. 6%
38. car payment
39. transportation
40. household
41. rent
42. savings
43. car payment
44. car payment
45. vacation
46. food
47. personal
48. savings
49. food, housing, transportation
50. food, $\frac{4}{25}$; housing, $\frac{3}{10}$;

clothing, $\frac{3}{50}$; savings, $\frac{1}{8}$; transportation, $\frac{1}{5}$; entertainment, $\frac{1}{20}$; medical care, $\frac{1}{20}$; other, $\frac{11}{200}$

51. Possible answer: decimals; using fractions would require rewriting them with a common denominator.

52. food, 15%; housing, 32%; clothing, 9%; savings, 14%; transportation, 7%; entertainment, 8%; medical care, 9%; other, 6%

53. food, housing, savings

54. housing, food, savings, clothing = medical care, entertainment, transportation, other

Pages 60-62
Think About It
1. Inflation causes these costs to rise over time.

2. Possible answer: Start a college savings fund as soon as a child is born.

Practice
1. $9,000
2. $12,000
3. $67,000
4. $19,000
5. $9,000
6. $13,000
7. $74,000
8. $21,000
9. $10,000
10. $13,000
11. $78,000
12. $22,000
13. $10,000
14. $13,000
15. $82,000
16. $23,000

17. $211,710
18. $231,390
19. $529,740
20. $551,410
21. $200,370
22. $205,960
23. $469,990
24. $239,520
25. $294,540
26. $217,620
27. $315,000
28. $40,680
29. $236,410
30. $214,430

Pages 64-66
Think About It
1. The net worth of a homeowner will often be higher than the net worth of a renter because the value of a house typically tends to rise as the years pass.

2. Net worth is not a good indicator of available money because some types of assets cannot be easily spent.

Practice
1. $7,784
2. $124,083
3. $193,500
4. $6,750
5. $6,660
6. $215,636
7. $143,969
8. $71,667
9. $215,400
10. $29,900
11. $7,271
12. $169,083
13. $260,165

14. $44,529
15. $188,969
16. $45,000
17. $71,196
18. $3,375
19. $2,034
20. $1,236
21. $8,540
22. $132,870
23. $152,038
24. $69,545
25. $82,493
26. $162,998
27. $81,505
28. $81,493

Page 68
Decision Making
(Some answers may vary. Accept reasonable answers based on students' rationales.)

1. $472
2. Limited
3. No
4. $400
5. Limited
6. Yes
7. $250
8. Excellent
9. Excellent
10. Good
11. Good
12. Yes
13. $300
14. Limited
15. Limited
16. Yes

17. Any two of the following: Science Fair aid, Health Fair, Greenhouse, Trees

18. Health Fair, Greenhouse

19. Bus trip, Health Fair

20. Answers will vary. Possible answers: beauty, shade

21. Answers will vary. Possible answers: studying plants, growing plants to sell

22–24. Answers will vary.

Check students' graphs.

Page 70
Decision Making
1. $1,587
2. $1,772
3. $1,089
4. $1,014
5. $3,679
6. $3,427
7. $3,167
8. $3,427
9. 0
10. 0
11. 0 hours
12. About 15.5 hours
13. 0 hours
14. About 4 hours
15. Plan A
16. Plan A
17. Plan B
18. $252
19–21. Answers may vary.

Pages 71-72
Money Tips
1. 1600%
2. about 686%
3. Possible answers: being signed by the artist; being in good condition
4. Possible answer: Items would increase in value if the demand for them exceeds the supply. Items that have special significance (because of its owner or creator, or because of its historical importance) might also increase in value.
5. Answers will vary.
6. Possible answer: Do research on the Internet, or have the items appraised by experts, professional collectors, or dealers in sports collectibles. Valuable items could be stored in a vault or safety deposit box or lent to a museum.
7. Answers will vary.

Pages 73-74
Calculator Practice
1. 50%
2. 25%
3. 500%
4. 20%
5. 6,000%
6. 300%
7. 2.6%
8. 744%
9. 25%
10. 12.5%
11. 9%
12. 84%
13. 15%
14. 114%
15. 22%
16. 74%

Pages 75-76
Part II Review:
1. a
2. a
3. c
4. a. $3.40
   b. $51.90
5. a. $1.24
   b. $15.79
6. 6.9%
7. 8.1%
8. $17,266
9. $29,542.50
10. $425
11. $84
12. $486
13. housing and transportation
14. $208
15. $71
16. $2,055
17. $518
18. $223,680
19. $481,830
20. $203,026
21. $102,934
22. $100,092

Page 77
Part II Test
1. $1.04
2. $2.70
3. 9.2%
4. 20.9%
5. $19,010.50

6. $25,994.88
7. $57
8. $425
9. $591
10. $3,050
11. $66
12. 35%
13. $12,000
14. $193,716
15. $102,160
16. $91,556

Part III: Investments
pp. 79-80
Pre-Skills Test
1. $287.50
2. $37.23
3. $64.32
4. $2,384.24
5. $2.32
6. $2.17
7. $5.46
8. $5.39
9. $500
10. $37.50
11. $126.16
12. $187.40
13. $132
14. $1,207.50
15. $16.50
16. $116
17. $28
18. $548
19. 200
20. 0.975
21. 0.925
22. $32.40
23. $43.20
24. $962
25. 0.75
26. 0.125
27. 0.5
28. 0.875
29. 0.0483
30. 0.0514
31. 0.0275
32. 0.03375
33. 5.4%
34. 5.35%
35. 3.94%
36. 99.75%
37. $218.75
38. $35.56
39. $230
40. $482.35
41. 17.5%
42. 98.4%
43. 27.1%
44. 121.8%

Pages 82-84
Think About It
1. The U.S. federal government pays the interest out of the money collected in federal taxes.
2. because you are lending money to the federal government when you buy a U.S. Savings Bond

Practice

1. $50	**2.** $37.50
3. $100	**4.** $500
5. $1,500	**6.** $12,500
7. $275	**8.** $289.80
9. $2,974	**10.** $569.20
11. $54.08	**12.** $43.47
13. $839.40	**14.** $89.40
15. $113.84	**16.** $13.84
17. $1,210.40	**18.** $210.40
19. $144.90	**20.** $19.90
21. $24,624	**22.** $4,624
23. $230.94	**24.** $5.94
25. $40,572	**26.** $5,572
27. $170.76	**28.** $20.76
29. $424.96	**30.** $24.96
31. $579.60	**32.** $79.60
33. $223.05	**34.** $35.55

35. $3,357.60

36. $357.60

37. $11,384

38. $1,384

39. $15,130

40. $2,630

41. a. $250
 b. $265.60
 c. $297.40
 d. $31.80

42. a. $50
 b. $61.56
 c. $100
 d. $38.44

Pages 86-88
Think About It

1. When a customer buys a CD, the bank knows how long it will have access to those funds and how long before it will have to redeem the CD. By contrast, a customer can withdraw funds from a savings account at any time. For these reasons, banks are willing to pay more interest on CDs.

2. Possible answer: because interest rates may go up while their money is tied up in a CD and they would be subject to a penalty if they withdraw their money early

Practice

1. 0.60%	**2.** 1.85%
3. 2.40%	**4.** 1.00%
5. $31.25	**6.** $12.50
7. $75	**8.** $30
9. $18.75	**10.** $100

11. a. $150
 b. $150
 c. $300

12. a. $187.50
 b. less; $112.50

13. a. $30
 b. $30
 c. $60

14. a. $50
 b. less; $10

Extension

1. 2.3%	**2.** 1.4%
3. 3.2%	**4.** 2.8%
5. 3.0%	**6.** 2.4%

7. a. 1.3%
 b. 1.0%
 c. the CD

Pages 91-92
Think About It

1. The prices of stocks fluctuate in response to supply and demand. When more people want to buy than to sell, the price goes up. When more people want to sell than to buy, the price goes down.

2. A "bull" market is a strong market with stock prices moving up, while a "bear" market is a weak market with stock prices moving down.

Practice

1. $18.00	**2.** $30.75
3. 108,000	**4.** $2.18
5. $2.52	**6.** $45.02
7. $28.87	

8. decrease of $0.13

9. EGadW, Enhart, EssWt

10. $1,014

11. $661.50

12. $3,986.25

13. $1,001

14. $4,062.50

15. $105,294

16. (P) $217.20

17. (L) $525.60

18. (P) $2,058

19. (L) $5,277.50

20. $0.56	**21.** $5.60
22. 1.6%	**23.** $1.80
24. $72	**25.** 4.8%
26. $0.72	**27.** $54
28. 1.7%	**29.** $0.28
30. $140	**31.** 1.8%

32. a. $634.75
 b. $154.75
 c. $4

Page 94
Problem Solving Applications

1. $8.23	**2.** $86.50
3. $57.14	**4.** $87.06
5. increase	**6.** increase
7. decrease	**8.** decrease

Support Materials
The Mathematics of Personal Finance and Investment, SV 9780547625683

9. Nostro 10. Nasco
11. 3 stocks 12. Nostro
13. $9.13 high; $6.85 low
14. $2.28
15. $420
16. no
17. (P) $162

Pages 97-98
Think About It
1. Stocks represent a piece of ownership in a corporation, while bonds represent only a loan to a corporation or government. Stocks pay dividends, while bonds pay interest.
2. Municipal bonds are issued by local governments, while corporate bonds are issued by corporations.

Practice
1. Chapman International
2. Chapman International
3. City of Yuma
4. Chapman International
5. City of Yuma, Dover Products
6. Chapman International, Eastern Metals, Finch Township
7. $3,812 8. $8,032
9. $20,440 10. $13,365
11. 95% 12. 87.5%
13. 83.75% 14. 150%
15. 105% 16. 112.5%
17. $510 18. $413
19. $1,590 20. $2,625
21. 7.1% 22. 4.6%
23. 8.1% 24. 5.2%

Pages 100-102
Think About It
1. Because mutual funds represent a broad array of investments, investing in mutual funds is usually less risky than buying and selling individual stocks and bonds. Their earnings, or yields, are often higher than most individuals would be likely to get by themselves.

Practice
1. $38.12 2. $1,906
3. $9,530 4. $17.18
5. $859 6. $4,295
7. $15.28 8. $764
9. $3,820 10. $24.12
11. $1,206 12. $6,030
13. $4,124 14. $14,340
15. $5,637.50 16. $278
17. $33,154 18. $9,622.50
19. $515.40 20. $3,105.90
21. 509 shares
22. 729 shares
23. 106 shares
24. $832
25. $2,964
26. $16
27. $13.68
28. $684
29. $3,420
30. $16.09
31. $804.50
32. $4,022.50
33. $16.61
34. $830.50
35. $4,152.50
36. $1,846
37. $22,752
38. $663.50
39. $4,983
40. 365 shares
41. $1,117.50

Pages 106-108
Think About It
1. Because pension fund contributions are invested and earn interest, the fund grows as much from investment income as from ongoing employee contributions.
2. Possible answer: An employee with a 401(k) plan may get matching contributions to the plan from his or her employer. With an IRA, an individual does not get employer contributions.
3. Possible answer: If a person will be in a lower tax bracket when retired, he or she might pay less in taxes on withdrawals from a traditional IRA than on contributions made now to a Roth IRA.

Practice
1. 2.00
2. $9,600
3. $800
4. 1.41
5. $7,994.70
6. $666.23
7. 1.89
8. $13,475.70
9. $1,122.98
10. 1.79
11. $8,559.78
12. $713.32
13. 2.00
14. $16,575
15. $1,381.25

16. $1,500
17. $62.50
18. $2,667
19. $222.25
20. $4,240
21. $81.54
22. $2,632
23. $219.33
24. $1,180
25. $45.38
26. $810
27. $405
28. $1,675
29. $837.50
30. $2,172
31. $1,086
32. $3,528
33. $1,764
34. $3,200
35. $5,000
36. $300
37. $1,000
38. a. 1.88
    b. $20,106.60
    c. $1,675.55
39. a. $4,620
    b. $385
40. a. $1,680
    b. $420
    c. $2,100

Pages 110-112
Problem Solving Strategy
Think About It

1. Find the amount that Roy has: (a) at the end of the 14th year, so it would triple to be $108,000 at the end of the 21st year; (b) at the end of the 7th year, so it would triple to be $36,000 at the end of the 14th year; and (c) at the beginning of the 1st year, so it would triple to be $12,000 at the end of the 7th year.

2. $4,000

Practice

1. $20,000	2. $10,000
3. $22,500	4. $11,250
5. $27,000	6. $9,000
7. $3,000	8. $18,000
9. $6,000	10. $2,000
11. $25,000	12. $9,000
13. $9,375	14. $27,000
15. $8,750	16. $12,500
17. $10,000	18. $17,500

Pages 114-116
Decision Making

1. $37.50	2. 0.5%
3. 15.4% (I)	4. High
5. $87.37	6. $2.75
7. 3.1%	8. 18.6% (D)
9. None	10. 0%
11. 14.8% (I)	12. Moderate
13. $15.25	14. $1.75
15. 41.9% (I)	16. Low
17. $117.75	18. $4.50
19. 3.8%	20. Low
21. $21.50	22. $1.00
23. 4.7%	24. 16.2% (I)
25. High	26. Techno

27. Jetstorm
28. Laserpert
29. Laserpert
30. Laserpert
31. Phantom
32. Laserpert and Jetstorm; low risk
33. Approximately 12 shares of Jetstorm and 69 shares of Phantom
34. Answers may vary.

35. $22.50	36. 4.4%
37. 9.8% (I)	38. High
39. $75.67	40. $2.25
41. 3.0%	42. 19.6% (D)
43. None	44. 0%
45. 11.4% (I)	46. Low
47. $124.25	48. $4.50
49. 2.4% (D)	50. High
51. $16.50	52. $2.00
53. 12.1%	54. Low
55. $39.45	56. $0.60
57. 1.5%	58. 11.3% (I)

59. Moderate
60. NeoElec 61. Franklin
62. Tor G & E
63. Tor G & E
64. Tor G & E
65. State Gas
66. NeoElec and Tor G & E; low risk
67. Approximately 106 shares of Tor G & E and 23 shares of Ray G & E
68. Approximately 106 shares of Tor G & E and 44 shares of New Gas
69. Answers may vary.

Pages 117-118
Money Tips

1. Possible answers: To provide for a more comfortable retirement; to protect earnings from taxes; to invest in a plan that may earn at a rate higher than other investments would offer

2. Possible answers: Less earned income (self-employed persons' income usually varies from year to year); higher expenses; money used for more immediate

needs (car, home repair, a new baby)

3. $72,000

4. a. $2,000

   b. $3,200

   c. $4,800

5. Self-employed persons who make tax-deductible contributions to a Keogh profit-sharing plan would pay less in federal tax than they otherwise would.

6. Possible options: (a) Invest the 10%, pay your expenses, and live on a more limited budget; (b) Invest the 10% and cut down expenses where possible; (c) Invest less, say 5%, to reduce the financial burden; or (d) Invest nothing for that year. Answers will vary as to which option to choose.

7. Answers may vary.

Page 120
Estimation Skill

(Estimates may vary. Possible estimates given.)

1. 3,500⁻

2. 9,000⁺

3. 18,000

4. $90⁻

5. $40

6. $600⁺

7. 36⁺

8. 140⁻

9. 40

10. 20⁻

11. 20⁺

12. 50⁺

13. $2⁻

14. $3⁻

15. $8⁻

16. 3⁺

Pages 122-124
Problem Solving Strategy

1. b

2. a

3. Possible estimate: $25; exact answer: $24.75

4. Possible estimate: $9,000; exact answer: $8,525

5. Possible estimate: $40,000; exact answer: $39,312

6. Possible estimate: $9,000; exact answer: $8,635

7. Possible estimate: $2,200; exact answer: $2,266

8. Possible estimate: $45; exact answer: $45.75

9. Possible estimate: $12,000; exact answer: $10,696

10. Possible estimate: $3,500; exact answer: $3,055.50

11. Possible estimate: $60; exact answer: $62.92

Pages 125-126
Part III Review

1. b

2. a

3. c

4. $139.67

5. $17.84

6. $2,136

7. $28,065

8. $407.10

9. $2,139

10. 5.9%

11. 7.2%

12. $64.92

13. $3,163.20

14. $22,800

15. $9,180

16. $160

17. $3,600

18. $8,000

19. $1,772.86

Pages 127-128
Part III Test

1. $315.60 (P)

2. $264 (L)

3. $963.60 (P)

4. $865.50 (L)

5. $777.80

6. $20.40

7. $7,415

8. $11.09 per share

9. $116.85

10. $51 profit

11. $58.31

12. $403.50

13. $1,306.67

14. $1,200

15. $12,000

16. $7,680

17. $68.97

18. $8.70

19. stock

20. $69

CPSIA information can be obtained
at www.ICGtesting.com
Printed in the USA
LVHW060839190723
752810LV00011B/534